CHURCH REFORM:

THE ONLY MEANS TO THAT END,

STATED IN

A LETTER

TO

Sir ROBERT PEEL, Bart.

FIRST LORD OF THE TREASURY, &c.

By RICHARD CARLILE.

TO WHICH IS PREFACED

A

CORRESPONDENCE WITH THE BISHOP OF LONDON ON THE SAME SUBJECT.

London:

PRINTED & PUBLISHED BY R. CARLILE, 62, FLEET STREET.

1835.

PREFACE.

CORRESPONDENCE WITH THE BISHOP OF LONDON,
IN 1833,
ON THE SUBJECT OF A
REFORM IN THE CHURCH.

" *To the Right Reverend Father in God, the Lord Bishop of London.*

         " 62, Fleet Street, November 18, 1833.

" MY LORD,

  " I have long and deliberately thought, that the state of the Country, the state of the Church, and the state of the Public Mind in relation to the Church, calls upon me to offer myself for an interview with your Lordship, as my Diocesan, that your Lordship may hear from me what I have to advance against the present state and condition of the Church, and what I have to propose as an immediately necessary and proper Reform.

  " I offer to wait on your Lordship, with your Lordship's consent; and promise, that my conversation shall be altogether courteous and reasonable.

      " I am one of your Lordship's scattered sheep,
       wishing for the fold of a good shepherd,—
       (which is Christ Jesus),—
        " RICHARD CARLILE."

  " P. S.—I may add, my Lord Bishop, that I am altogether a Christian; save the mark at which superstition has been planted upon Christianity."

" *To Mr. R. Carlile.*

" SIR,

" I have to acknowledge the receipt of your letter, in which you propose an interview with me, for the purpose of making known to me your opinions respecting the present state of the Church.

" I beg to say, that I shall be ready to receive, and to give all due consideration to any communication which you may think proper to make me in writing ; as being, on many accounts, a more convenient method than that of personal conference.

" I remain, SIR,

" Your obedient Servant,

" C. J. LONDON."

" *To the Right Reverend Father in God, the Lord Bishop of London.*

" 62, Fleet Street, November 24, 1833.

" MY LORD BISHOP,

" In answer to my proposal to meet your Lordship in conversation, on the state of the Country, the state of the Church, and the state of the Public Mind with relation to the Church, your Lordship has encouraged me to write what I have to say, and has promised to receive it and to give it due consideration. I write as early as my circumstances have afforded me the necessary leisure and composure of mind.

" The first point to which I beg leave to call your Lordship's attention is— that there is a very numerous degree of dissent from the Established Church among the people of this country.

" The second point is, that this spirit of dissent has led to a very extended opposition to the support of the Church in its fiscal claims.

" The third point is, that there is a preparation of a public mind going forward for the putting of the present Established

Church on the same footing as the present Establishments of the Dissenters—the footing of voluntary rather than legal support; and that the preparation of this state of mind is accelerated by the embarrassed state of the country.

" The evidence of these three points in prospect is, that the present state of the Church will be entirely overthrown in the course of two or three Sessions of Parliament.

" On the principle of dissent from the Established Church, I have to observe, that it is desirable there should be no dissent; but then the Church should be invulnerable. There can be no popular dissent from any Institution that can be defended as good and best; and though I am instructed to allow that the general body of dissenters from the Church have dissented on very frivolous, even on indefensible grounds, (inasmuch as the Dissenters have not corrected in themselves the errors of the Church), there still remains the proof that where the Church has been assailed or dissented from, it has not been in a condition to defend and justify itself.

" This incapability of the Church to defend and justify itself, where assailed, must have arisen from a defective state of its doctrine and discipline.

" This doctrine and discipline is founded upon the literal reading of the Sacred Scriptures, or the books of the Old and New Testament.

" I impugn the literal as an erroneous reading: it claims to be local and temporal history, and is not. Not one of its apparent historical subjects can be verified. Every one of them can be falsified, upon the principle that other things were being done at the time, and that other people dwelt in the places; and that nothing of contemporary character, purporting to be history, has corroborated the historical claims of the Old and New Testament.

" It is said of the writings of the Old and New Testament, that they are allegorical, and that they contain the moral of human salvation from evil. Under this view, they may be true, and may be important as a matter of instruction. I so believe them to be true, and to be important as a matter of instruction; but as your Lordship may put me on the task of mentioning

some particular facts and grounds on which I impugn the literal
reading of the Sacred Scriptures, and may properly suggest that
it is necessary this ground should be first cleared before we try
them on the other ground, I submit, as two well-weighed and
conclusive propositions :—

"1st. That the person of Jesus Christ, or the name, is not
in mention by any author of the first century, if the passage in
Josephus be excepted as an interpolation ; and that this defect
in the evidence is fatal to the historical claim.

" 2nd. That the people called Jews, or Israelites, neither
formed colony nor nation in that part of the earth which is now
called Judea, or Holy Land, before the time of Alexander of
Macedon ; consequently all that is said of their dwelling in and
going out of Egypt, their sojourn in the Wilderness, their warfare with the Canaanites and Philistines, their occupation of
that country, their subsequent conquest, captivity, and restoration, is entirely fiction or allegory.

" I read it as political and moral instruction veiled in allegory ; and as it is to be desired, that, in the removal of a
system, all its defects be made apparent, so it becomes a desideratum, that we account for the origin of the sects named Jews
and Christians.

" This may be done in two ways—one, that they were public
philosophical sects ; the other, that they were degrees of order
in the ancient mysteries.

" The moral of the allegory belonging to each is throughout
the same, and is an encouragement to the resistance and overthrow of the tyranny of man, when it appears in the open
authority of a King, or in the covert authority of a Priest ; and
the preparing of a people to do this, and the doing it, is precisely
what is meant by human salvation,—which is a sure and certain
salvation from earthly evils.

" The absence of a proof of personal identity in the characters
sketched in the Old and New Testament, is the presence of proof
(if utility of any kind there be in the form of the allegory), that
the persons mentioned are like what all the gods and goddesses
of ancient religion were—personifications of principles, either
physical or moral, or both.

" In so receiving the Scriptures of the Old and New Testament, I find them pregnant with the most important political and moral instruction. In receiving them according to the literal or historical reading, I find difficulties insuperable, and such as justify all that Thomas Paine or any other straightforward critic has advanced on the subject, while the moral and the allegory were concealed from their view.

" The point at which this personification of principles begins, is the point at which superstition begins; for though knowledge may justify the poetic licence taken with language, ignorance mistakes and evil design misrepresents, until the personification is extensively dwelt on as a reality.

" Here I trace the fundamental errors of the present doctrine and discipline of the Established Church; the errors upon which dissent has progressed, upon which an outcry of infidelity has been raised, but upon which the Church could not defend itself and maintain its position.

" My remedy for the present difficulties, and my proposition for a Reform in the Church is, that no difficulties, mysteries, or superstition be allowed to remain attached to its doctrines and discipline; that the allegory of the Sacred Scriptures be avowed, the personifications taught upon their principles as known principles of nature, and not as personified incomprehensibilities; that the Church, in short, be made a school for the people, than which, if it originally meant any good thing, could mean no other thing, where from time to time all acquired or acquirable knowledge should be taught. On this ground, the utility of the Iustitution is evident, the benefit to the people certain, the idea of dissent inadmissible.

" In this first letter, I have thought it necessary only to give your Lordship the leading points of objection to the present doctrine and discipline of the Church. With details in proof, I can proceed to a voluminous length; and I now offer myself to submit to the catechism of your Lordship, or to that of any person whom your Lordship shall appoint to see me, with the distinct promise, that I will not evade the giving of a direct answer to any distinct and intelligible question that can be put to me upon any part of this important subject.

" It may not be improper that I now declare to your Lordship, that, after having worn out the spirit of persecution by a
large amount of personal and pecuniary suffering, I have never
been acting upon any other motive than a love of truth, and
honesty, and public good ; that it is under such a motive, and
no other mixed motive, that I have now presented myself to
your Lordship, viewing your Lordship as a public functionary
that has inherited and not created the error of which I complain ; and hoping that I shall be met with the disposition of
a fair investigation, when so much good is at this moment the
promised consequence,

" I am, MY LORD,

" Your Lordship's most obedient humble servant,

" RICHARD CARLILE."

A LETTER, &c.

Sir,

I write as a politician to a politician, with oblivion of the past, without any profession of respect for the present, waiting and watching your future.

I am stimulated to address you, and the country through your name, on reading your Address to the Electors of Tamworth, after taking the offices of First Lord of the Treasury and Chancellor of the Exchequer.

The portion of your Address which I select as my subject, is that relating to the Church— the first of all political subjects. Not to understand how to deal with this, is to be utterly deficient in every other political branch. Not to reform this, is to reform nothing. State ever did, and ever will, depend upon the Church.

As far as your individual promise is sufficient, it is, that Church Rates shall be abolished. This is so far good. It has been a disgrace to all parties concerned, and an injury to every housekeeper, that a Church Rate has existed. Such a rate has existed only because of the dishonest application of that Church Property

B

which was the legitimate supply for all Church Buildings and repairs. And should the rate be continued under any other form of taxation, and not supplied from existing Church Property, an injury and an injustice will still be inflicted upon the people.

You seem willing to abate the religious ceremony of marriage, so far as to allow each couple to let it be to its liking. Pray go a step farther, and let the law cease to trammel that civil contract with religious ceremony, while each couple will be at liberty of its own accord to go through whatever religious ceremony it may think proper. And while on this subject, I pray you to give, or seek for the poor, justice in facile divorce. The mystery of marriage is too sacred for constraint. It should never be other than a spirit of pure and mutual liberty and consent, subject to some legal recognition for the care of offspring. Much of the morals of society must depend on the freedom of marriage and facility of divorce. We have not hitherto been right on this subject. That can be no good tie which opposes the will of an individual in so sacred and delicate an affair as that of marriage. The beginning, middle, and end of marriage should be the love of affection and friendship. Marriage should cease when affection between the parties has ceased. It may be truly added, that marriage has morally ceased, when affection has ceased. Then the legal tie becomes an abomination, a source of vice and wrong; and, in nine cases out of ten, the religious ceremony is treated as a burlesque, save the idea, that it is a fashionable distinction to have observed it as the chief criterion of legal marriage.

I entirely agree with you, that Church Property should not be alienated from strictly ecclesiastical purposes. I have changed my view, and see more than formerly on this head.

For the same reason, I entirely disagree with you on any commutation of tithes. Let the original application be restored, and no one will find fault but he who loses by that just principle, that first and best of Church Property, and most important of popular rights.

The point, in your address, on which my letter is to be based, is the following paragraph :—

" With regard to alterations in the laws which govern our ecclesiastical establishment, I have had no recent opportunity of giving that grave consideration to a subject of the deepest interest, which could alone justify me in making any public declaration of opinion. It is a subject which must undergo the fullest deliberation, and into that deliberation the Government will enter with the sincerest desire to remove every abuse that can impair the efficiency of the Establishment, extend the sphere of its usefulness, and to strengthen and confirm its just claims upon the respect and affections of the people."

This is just what I wanted you to say. It is honest, if you will but act up to it. This is the sort of Church Reform that I propose. Here

we have from you, as the Chief Minister, a promise that your Administration will enter into
the fullest deliberation, with the sincerest desire
to remove every abuse that can impair the
efficiency of the Church Establishment, extend
the sphere of its usefulness, and strengthen
and confirm its just claims upon the respect
and affections of the people. Had I been called
to your situation, I could not have promised
more; but I should have acted up to that promise, and I hope you will so act. In the performance of that promise, everlasting fame will
be yours. So act—and greater than the name
of Lycurgus or Solon—greater than that of
Cicero, Constantine, or Napoleon—greater than
the name of any past man will be that of
Robert Peel. If the Duke of Wellington join
you in this sentiment, and goes manly and
honestly forward to its accomplishment, his,
too, will be an imperishable name. This would
wreathe him an evergreen chaplet, that would
survive the memory of all his physical victories!
This is the great moral victory to be obtained
before any society can settle down into peace,
welfare, and happiness :—*the best use that can
be made of the Church.* It is a subject of the
deepest interest ; it requires grave consideration ; I pray that it may have that consideration. I pray that I may be heard by a Commission, in grave consideration of that subject

of the deepest interest, before any legislative change be entered upon. I put myself forward in this letter. Many will be the schemes proposed to your consideration : let mine be one, and then select and improve the best.

The first consideration is—What is now the Church? What are its defects? What the cause of that dissent, which has made a revision necessary?

The second consideration will be—What ought the Church to be, so as to leave no ground and reason of dissent? To some minds, the fickleness and fallibility of human nature will appear as an insurmountable obstacle to the construction of such a Church. I see farther and will propose in order.

I flatter myself that I am writing this letter with very proper feelings toward all institutions and all persons. I suspend, *pro tem.*, all quarrels that I have with all men, to assist you in this common good, in which you deserve and will have, in the ratio of their goodness, the assistance of all good men. If I can sink the past in oblivion for common good, who should say he cannot? To the altar and shrine of that Reformed Church, which you contemplate, I have sacrificed property much—all I had, and years of liberty many. I am still worshipping, still so sacrificing, both property and personal liberty, and will so continue to the end. I say it not boastfully; but in comparative claim to attention, and in encouragement and example of union to assist you in the performance of your present promise.

Let me be permitted to say, too, that the Church is a subject which I have studied in its origin, its history, its first principle, all its dissent or variation from that first principle, down to its present standing. I have so studied it, that I cannot now find author or preacher who can present me any thing new as to its general merits, past or present. This is the chief ground on which I solicit your and the public attention to my view of this subject of Church Reform. I presume to know what the Church is, and what it ought to be.

It may be taken as a point to be yielded by all parties, that the desire with regard to the Law Established Church is, the removal of all ground of dissent, so as not to leave it a mere sectarian Church, which any mere abatement of existing dissenting objections will do. No Dissenter can complain, if the ground of his dissent be removed from the Church. And if there be no ground of future dissent left, there can be no future complaint, no new dissension arising. Without the absence of the possibility of dissent, there can be no just holding and application of a public and common property for the business of the Church. With that absence, the property is justly held and applied. Any law that recognizes and tolerates the Dissenter, recognizes and tolerates the justness of his dissent, and calls for the primary justice of removing the ground of dissent. No man can reasonably say, *let us not be of one Church;* but every man can reasonably say, *let the Church be purified of its errors;* and while any man can show an error, it is his duty to call for the purification, and the duty of authorities to attend to his call and to purify. A permanent Church then must be an improving, self-purifying Church, and continue a true picture of the best state of the human mind, meeting every well-founded and majority-decided call upon its utility.

Any idea of keeping up a Law Established Church with public property, surrounded by Dissenting Churches, without a public property, can enter the head of no man who understands the subject. There can be no peace or final settlement under such an arrangement. The effect to be accomplished is, not to break up the Church Property; but to break up the Dissenters from the Church. This will startle the present state of mind and feeling. I propose no abridgement of equal liberty. Is not this the grand *desideratum?* Can it be accomplished?— I think it can, and so proceed to unfold the two-fold consideration.

First.—What is now the Church ? What are its defects? What the cause of that dissent which has made a revision necessary ?

This, in reality, is but one question, with a three-fold expression.

The Church is now the Theatre of the Drama of the Books of Common Prayer, the Thirty-nine Articles, and the Old and New Testament ; to which is generally added a sermonic epilogue or exhortation, commonly called a Sermon.

Be not offended at my use of the word *Theatre* here : no other would substitute. Its root is the Greek Θεὸς, God, and signified originally, the house, place or stage, where the Drama of Theism or attributes of Deity were exhibited. The word is now much distorted from its root, in being made to describe the place of modern dramatic performances.

Nor must the word *Drama* be objected to ; because the ceremony of the Church was originally so constructed, so meant, and so practised, as I will prove in the course of this letter.

Even the word *Tragedy* has its root in the Greek word τραγος, a goat, and signifies, in the dramatic exhibition of Theism, the death of the year, under the form of a personification, in the twelfth or zodiacal month of the goat. So that the death sorrowed for and lamented, was, dramatically, the apparent death of the sun, the death of the year, in the sign or month of the goat; and on St. Thomas's day, as we read in the Prophet Ezekiel, chap. viii. v. 14—"*and behold there sat women weeping for Tammuz ;*" and v. 16—"*about five and twenty men, with their backs toward the temple of the Lord, and their faces toward the east ; and they worshipped the sun toward the east,*" which is no other than a representation of the performance of the tragedy, in which the performers had lost the moral of the Lord's Temple : precisely the present state and condition of the Church. All ancient mythology is in harmony with this conclusion ; and the Christian tragedy is only a continued version, uniting the general drama of human morals with the annual tragedy of solar physics, and forming a two-fold or two-keyed allegory or mystery, physical and moral, as it was known even in the Celtic or Druid Church. Christianity was never new, or young, in this country, by existing records.

There are not many persons in this secret, perhaps, not even you, the first Minister of the country ; so it will be deemed too abstruse and mystical on which to find a warrant for legislation or change of law ; but I strenuously maintain, that such was the origin of the Christian Church, and such is now its generally lost meaning. The proof of the solar part of the allegory is not so much to my present purpose as the proof of the general drama of human morals being the basis of the present mystery of the Christian Church.

To stay a growing difficulty, we must go to the root :—it will grow again, if we do not go to the root. It will be so with the present Church, and all attempts to reform it.

In plainer language, then, I will describe the existing Church, as having, in its ceremonies and business, the mystery of the Christian Religion, without its revelation ; that all the defects and all the grounds of dissent from it are the absence of the revelation, or want of knowing the meaning of the mystery. Whatever are called its doctrines, are all mysterious ; its discipline is equally mysterious, and by its present ministers, unaccountable. Dissenters have dissented without being able to assign a reason for their dissent, and have set up for themselves something equally mysterious and unaccountable ; and so the whole principle and practice of Religion in the country is in confusion and conflict ; and no measure can reconcile the dissentients, short of developing the first principles of the Church and the Christian Religion, the one language, the one course of reason, the one ground of human welfare, the one system of morals, which is now buried in a Babel of confused tongues, doctrines, idol-houses, and superstitious ceremonies.

The ground, then, on which I proceed, is,

that TO REFORM THE CHURCH, THE
DISSENTERS MUST BE ANNIHILATED.
Not annihilated by slaughter or physical force;
but by superior knowledge, and consequent
superior teaching, by openness, by honesty, by
throwing off the mask of hypocrisy, and leaving
the Church of Christ to be no longer a theatre
of dramatic ceremony in mystery, with parts
and actors as ignorant as automata of their
subject, and who not knowing, can value it not,
beyond the salaries they receive for its performance in unrevealed mystery.

Can that be a Reform of the Church, with
"just claims upon the respect and affections of
the people," which shall leave a ground and
excuse for dissent by any one of the people?
I say, NO. Can it be a Church of Christ? I
say, NO. Do we know what a Church of
Christ is in reality? For myself, I say, YES.
A Church, too, founded upon an understanding
of the *Sacred* Scriptures, of the Old and New
Testament, upon the revelation of the mystery
of those Scriptures, and upon all the first principles essential and conducive to general human
and social welfare; that shall no more admit of
dissent than the multiplication table, or the
accurately placed sun-dial, than the elements of
Euclid, and all the never-failing tests of the
science of chemistry. The Apostle that told us
to " *prove all things, and hold fast that which is*

good," gave us a definition of the exhortation of the Evangelist or the Baptist—"*Repent, for the kingdom of Heaven is at hand.*" A repenting and a proving people are necessary to make a Church of Christ. Repentance and enquiry are the pillars and foundations of that Church; without repentance and enquiry there can be no Church of Christ; and I ask, confidently ask, with the assurance that a true answer must be in the negative,—has anything calling itself a Christian Church in Europe, established by law, or dissenting from such an establishment, anything to do with the two principles of *repentance* and *proving*, the one meaning *reflection* by animadversion, the other a *trial by outward tests* of that reflection? There is not a congregation of people in Europe, calling itself a Church, that is founded upon an understanding of the Sacred Scriptures, the understanding which shows that the " letter killeth, but the spirit giveth life."

I impugn, as being in error,—I denounce, as that error is the cause of all dissent, of dissent uninstructed,—all the churches or congregations called churches in the British dominions; and I call for a reform that shall eradicate that dissent, and make all become one in efficiency, usefulness, and respect and affections of the people.

The present state of the Church is, that it is a theatre of mystery, giving no solid satisfaction to the people, and for which, among the receivers of salaries and benefits only, can there be a particle of real respect and affection. Its defects are, that none understand, neither priests nor people understand what any part of its dramatic ceremonies mean. And this is the cause of that dissent which has made a revision necessary.

What, then, ought the Church to be, so as to have no ground and reason of dissent?

In two words, I answer, A SCHOOL.

What kind of a school?

A school for knowledge only; for revelation without mystery; and for practical use and benefit to every member, without parade or pomp, even without ceremony, beyond what order and good may require.

And would such be a Church of Christ?

Such alone can be a Church of Christ. Christ the Logos, Jesus the Saviour of Man, is, in principle, nothing more in its dramatic or mystified and present church presentation, than a personification of the principle of reason, or of the knowledge of which the human being is a recipient, and without which can have no salvation, has no relation to the idea of a salvation, or any evil from which to be saved. Such is a true revelation of the mystery of Christ.

And a Church of Christ has no other true meaning, than a convenient and sessional ga-

14

thering of the people in districts, for purposes of mutual enquiry and mutual instruction ; for catechism and intelligible and useful exhortation ; for revelation of knowledge, or mind, or reason ; for mental improvement ; and not for mystery, nor dramatic ceremony, nor superstition, nor idolatry. It is in this sense only, that the Church of Christ is superior to all other Churches—the word *Church* meaning a gathering or association of the people for mental improvement.

This generation has no proof, nor has history a warrant, that any other generation of man has had a proof of the material existence of the being called Jesus Christ. The seeming narrative of such a purport is the current mythology of the ancients, or people of two thousand years ago, taken up by us in its literal sense, and so mistaken ; so mistaken, as to warrant a belief in the literality and fact of the material, temporal, and local existence of every one of the Gods of the Pantheon, or of human imagination, and then we shall have rivalry enough for the best. But then, I should make a choice of Christ, as the only one that makes due provision for the right cultivation of the human mind ; the only one that has laid the foundations of the kingdom of Heaven, in the peace and good-will of mankind, dwelling upon a land flowing with milk and honey, and overflowing with knowledge.

I challenge the Bishops and the whole priesthood, to produce me any knowledge that is
intelligible to themselves or to any other person,
as an interpretation of the narratives in the
Old and New Testament, about Jehovah or
Christ, other than that which I am now un-
folding. Mine has a warrant in the spirit of
the language of the books, in the roots of words,
and in all the principles of things that relate to
man's welfare; and more particularly in that to
man most important of all, MORAL SCIENCE.

I am not insensible to the circumstance, that
a man might have a knowledge of a thing, of a
train of circumstances, of causes and effects,
in his own mind, with a difficulty to find language in which to communicate it, that shall
be equally and immediately clear to all other
states of mind. A resemblance, nearness, or
similarity of mind, almost an equality of knowledge, is requisite to a clear understanding. It
is thus, that men, in different languages, understand each other, when other men, bystanders,
do not understand them. And it so happens,
in all first developments of science, the new
discovery wants a new language in which to be
presented to others, and it often happens, that
first words made or chosen are not the best and
clearest.

Know you not, Sir, that knowledge is power?
You must have read that celebrated axiom of

Bacon's; but have you considered it, have you reflected, have you repented and proved that axiom? I may add, by way of explanation, that knowledge is the only moral power. What seeks your Church to be? Or what should it seek to be, other than a moral power? On what rock, then, must the Church of Christ be built, so that the gates of hell, or of evil design, or of dissent, may not prevail against it? On what, but KNOWLEDGE? Is it now so built? Is not, rather, the present ministry of the Church more afraid of knowledge than of the people's ignorant dissent; more of " Carlile and his crew," than of all the dissenters; more of free discussion, than of any kind of superstition? The dissent of knowledge and the dissent of ignorance, though disunited, are becoming too powerful for your knowledgeless Church; and you, at last, have consented to speak of its necessary reform! To which will you yield, or whom will you join? Those who dissent by knowledge, or those by ignorance? If you take the former, your work will be perfected at once; if the latter, your work will never be done, and you will become weaker and weaker; for I know not one body of worshipping associated dissenters, whose ground of association and dissent is better than that of the Established Church. Find me the minister of one of them, who will stand up in discussion before a public audience with me, so as to have his language reported. I have not yet found him in England or Scotland. The pretences of the kind that have been made, have been so deficient in respectability of character and of good manners, that I do not think them worth a recognition.

I am not insensible to the circumstance, that you have a difficult task to perform, and I am not sure that you are equal to it: I hope you are; that is, I would have you so, or any other who may be the King's adviser, and the real head of the Church. Nothing is wanted for this reform but honesty and moral courage. Where the will and the power exist, the task is an easy one. *I desire to save the Church and its property, and to annihilate the Dissenters.* I would have the present dignities of the Church dignify themselves in a triumph over the Dissenters. A collusion with the Dissenters will be a hugging of pestilence and death to the bosom of the Church. There can be no co-existence: there was proof enough of that in the seventeenth century, and still in Scotland. A revolution in the affairs and manners of the Church must take place, even by your own confession, in language admitting of the inference; and I desire that good may be educed from that revolution. I would make the Church triumph in the correction of every mental error in the country, and noble would be that triumph!

You may ask, how is this to be done? I will tell you. Let the Church become the oracle of truth, the fountain of knowledge, the mistress and dispenser of all science. Let its ministers declare this great truth :—*that, hitherto, the mystery of Christ has alone been taught in the Church, without the revelation of that mystery ; that the Church has been the depository of that sacred mystery, until the fulness of time, in which it is promised, that all people shall be prepared to partake of the revelation ; that the mystery has been kept up in outward form and without any spiritual grace ; that the spiritual grace and all the promises are to be fulfilled in the understanding of the revelation ; that the spirit or revelation has been buried in a resting on the letter of the Sacred Scriptures ; that Christ is only now risen or beginning to rise, after thousands of years, we may say, three thousand years, rather than three days of crucifixion, death and burial.* In me, he has risen indeed, as, in me, he has been last crucified ; and I crave the pleasure of seeing his principles rise in the Church ; for that craving is the nature of Christ. Let the Church declare *that the time is now come to reveal the mystery of Christ.* Exhibition has not been revelation.

What, then, is the revelation of the mystery of Christ ?

It is, that Christ is God and not man, that it is God in man ; that it is knowledge, reason, or all its essences in moral principle; and that it is not an idol to be worshipped as a statue, but a principle to be taught and inherited by the human race. The mystery sets forth Christ as a statue or image to be worshipped after the fashion of the Pagan world. The revelation teaches, that it is the principle of knowledge, to be gained by labour, by asking, seeking and knocking, or prayer; by repentance, that is, reflection; by enquiry, that is, proving all things, and holding fast that which is good; by mutual instruction, by free discussion, by whatever constitutes a school for useful knowledge, and that constitution is a Church of Christ: all the rest is mistake or imposture, whether it be established by law, or ignorantly dissented from; whether it have a King for its head, or be carried on in a garret or a cellar.

I must go to the root of my subject, and leave no excuse for evasion. The root of religion is the relation of God to man, and man to God.

What does man know of God?

Books can teach him nothing, unless those books be written pictures of existing things, and things that have existed. Things that have existed have no source of trial or test, but in the similarity of things that do exist.

Man's knowledge of existence is of a two-fold nature: the things that do exist, and the power by which he has that knowledge. The first is distinguished as material existence; the second, as spiritual existence. Material and spiritual existence are the only two positive existences of which man can speak or write, to which no inspiration can add; for inspiration is only knowledge; and the recognition of material and spiritual existence is the limitation of knowledge. The details of knowledge can be nothing more than definitions and descriptions of existing things,—the plantings of art upon nature.

All knowledge is matter of art. Nature is the thing known—art the knowledge of the thing. This art can not only know nature, but can invent descriptions of unreal things; can describe things by types, and principles by figurative allegories; can imitate nature by appearances, such as pictures, statues, &c.; and can, by mysterious constructions of language, make the appearance of a thing to represent a principle or describe qualities in the absence of the thing: this is spiritual power. Nothing of the kind is seen beyond human life; certainly not beyond animal life. We may, therefore, reasonably speak of spiritual power or spiritual existence as confined to the human race—speech and language being a primary necessity to its existence: the art of other animals extending not beyond their wants.

Man, then, is the creator of spirit; and, beyond man, spirit is not known. Man is not known to be the creature, but the creator of art ; not the creature, but the creator of spirit, soul, mind, reason, knowledge, or whatever other term relates to the mental phenomena.

I maintain, because it is a truth of the deepest importance to the human race, and without the knowledge of which nothing can work well in human society, that man is the creator of all spiritual existence ; and in the sense in which God is a spirit, man is the creator of that God, and has been the creator of every description of existence that has been made of such a God.

We may also correctly speak of this two-fold existence as physical and moral. The physical, its forms and compositions excepted, is eternal and immutable—the moral is evanescent, mortal, and mutable in its personal existence, but immutable and immortal as to principle. The root of God, therefore, as of man, is in physical power, which is correctly described as almighty, immutable and omnipresent: it is only omniscient, as being the fountain of knowledge—the all that can be known. Science is art ; therefore, there can be no science in an infinite or eternal sense, as we can speak of the physical power of Deity ; but science, as art, is limited to human power,—the all that *is* known, and not the all that exists *to be* known.

This is evidence, that man has created not

only all the descriptions that have been made
of spiritual existence, but that existence itself:
and so it is true, that man has been the inventor
of a spiritual God; that religion and all its ap-
purtenances have been the offspring of the art
of man; and that man alone is capable of cor-
recting any of its errors,—which is to be done
in the same way by which I propose to put
down the Dissenters—the acquisition and communication of knowledge by the Church.

I pass by the Pagan mythology, which, in
its understood personifications and allegories,
is as beautiful a picture of physical and moral
nature, as the Christian Religion itself; and
I rest on the Christian, as, when understood,
the only religion for human improvement that
has been presented to the notice of the human
race.

As man is the inventor of the Spiritual Deity,
which is peculiarly the Deity of the Christian
Religion, so I infer, by evidence to come, that
the Deity of the Christian Religion is no other,
nothing more, than a personification of the
mental phenomena of the human race, which
was the work of the philosophers and scientific
men of the Pagan world: and noble was their
task—important for man was their production.
Not the thing called the Christian Religion now
in existence, which is no other than a religion
mistaken, a corruption and Pagan superstition,

the dregs and drivellings of the gross ignorance
and superstition of the dark ages; something
two thousand times worse than the Paganism
of the Millenium before the so-called Christian
era. But a personification after deifications of
the mental phenomena, is a sounding, preaching,
writing, carving or painting God, as the perfection of knowledge; Christ, as the perfection
of reason; and the Holy Spirit of communication, as the perfection of all attainable moral
power by the human race: making those per-
fections to be things sought, the things worshipped, the best religion, as it undoubtedly is,
for the whole human race. It was the best
plan of scholastic improvement, when acted
upon, that human wisdom could have devised;
and to this I would have you bring our Church.

There is a two-fold way of reading the Bible,
which I have before described, as it is described
in the Second Epistle to the Corinthians, chap.
iii. v. 6, a reading or a ministration according
to the letter, and another according to the spirit.
The Apostle or author of that Epistle declares
himself to have been a minister of the New
Testament according to the spirit, and com-
plains, that the Jews, in his time, did not know
how to read the Old Testament. I declare that
the Church now existing ministers to nothing
but the letter of the Bible, which is a ministration not to life, but to death; and such is the

evidence of the whole era of such a ministration; such has been the cause of the dark ages, on which no dissenting sect has yet thrown a ray of light; and the reform that is now required throughout the Church, that established by law and all others, *is the understanding of the Sacred Scriptures*, that shall cause them to be taught according to the spirit, the spirit of knowledge, reason and constant human improvement. I now see, that none of the people called Jews or Christians know how to read either Old or New Testament according to the spirit.

To read the Bible according to the letter, is to make it a piece of human history; to make a creation of the world, and an attempt to account for everything past, present and future. I proclaim this conduct to be the folly of ignorance, opposed by all real history of the human race, and by all the developments of science, in relation to the earth's existence, its qualities, and its relation to the general planetary system.

I challenge the proof of any one apparent historical fact, in either Old or New Testament. I challenge the production of the existing mention of any one of the supposed facts about the personal or material Jesus Christ, within one hundred years of the time at which it is said to have happened, putting the disputed passages of Josephus and Tacitus out of the question.

I challenge the proof of the existence of the

Jews, in any country, as a distinct nation, before the time of Alexander the Great.

No other contemporaneous history recognizes such an assumed history as that which I challenge.

And farther, I am prepared to prove that Christianity existed among Romans, Greeks, Persians, Hindoos, and Celtic Druids, or the northern nations, before the Christian era.

The present ministration of the Church entirely depends on the necessity of a clear historical proof of the literal contents of the Old and New Testaments.

But a spiritual reading of that volume solves every difficulty, and teaches us how to extract the truth, the system of religion that is a necessary and sure salvation for the human race, when reduced to practice, and to see it as a part of the wisdom of all ancient men of all times and countries.

It is ten years and upwards since I sent a petition to you, Sir, to be laid before the King, asking for a commission to examine my oppugnancy to the religion and administration of the existing Church. Will you now grant that commission? If you will not, you, while you remain in power, will blunder on in and through growing troubles and difficulties, until you, or some other person, be compelled to come to my school for information. It may be a galling pain, a conscience-smitten task to you to do so; but you have no alternative with honesty and wisdom. It is not a little of this cry for Church Reform, that has sprung out of my labours and sufferings. And here am I, though still in prison through that Church's iniquity, in the proud and triumphant position, clearly seeing that you can reform nothing in the Church that will satisfy the people without coming to my ground.

Your pledge is so to reform the Church as to make it meet the respect and affection of the people. I rejoiced when I read that sentiment; for I saw and felt, that I alone had proposed a reform equal to that end; and mine, as well as others, by the glorious power of the printing press, must come into consideration. I assure you that the correspondence with the Bishop of London, which I shall append to this letter, has been sold to the extent of many thousands, and is in great demand. This is but an enlargement of my second letter to the Bishop. So that my lamp has been constantly trimmed for your advent as a Reformer of the Church. It is not what you and others call "the rabble," "the destructives," "the mob," that I seek. I seek you and the Bishops, all the learned men in the country, as in application of mind to mind, learning to learning, and wisdom to wisdom.

I will now proceed to explain the distinction

between the mystery and the revelation of Christ, between the letter and the spirit of the books of the Old and New Testament, between false and true religion, between superstition and idolatry on one side, and reason with growing knowledge in the Church on the other. I begin with the doctrine of the Holy Trinity.

The Church of the dark ages has taught the doctrine professedly founded upon the letter of the Sacred Scriptures: of God, as consisting of three persons in one person, co-existent, co-equal, and co-eternal, which, in expression, has been abridged, under the name of Trinity, and described as the Holy Trinity; and, in definition or distinction, as Father, Son and Holy Ghost. This doctrine has always been dissented from while dissent has been tolerated. It is no more a physical absurdity than the doctrine of the resurrection of the dead, or the changing of water to wine, or the feeding of five thousand with five small loaves and two fishes, or any other narrated miracle: still it has been dissented from, and when dissented from, no defence could be made of it. In every other case of dissent, the Church could make no defence and no other apology than ancientness of the doctrine in the Church. Truly this has been a verification of the blind leading the blind, until both fell into the ditch together.

With a doctrine of personality in Deity, including the ideas of physical and moral power, this of the Trinity has been declared a mystery incomprehensible to the human mind; and I declare that a mystery incomprehensible to the human mind, pressed upon human attention, as of importance, is an absurdity, and must be an imposture; for who has comprehended it so to state? This is the matter-of-fact view of the subject.

But the subject being a declared mystery in the theological sense, there is a spiritual interpretation to be put upon the language of the letter; and that I take to be thus :—

That the Trinity is not to be considered as of persons, but of principles; and then we shall find it a philosophical doctrine, true to nature, and proved by science; true to physical and to moral science.

All the ideas that physical science can bring us of creation is the root of three in one. Whatever admits of analysis sets forth the truth and doctrine of the Trinity. Water, the great parent of production on this planet, is known to be composed of two gases—hydrogen and oxygen. They become water through contact and decomposition by electric action. Thus, in the order of a Trinity in Unity, we may describe it as of hydrogen, oxygen, electric contact=water. I do not mention this as any thing new; but it is new in application to a definition of the doctrine of the Trinity. Water had not been made but by the electric contact of hydrogen with oxygen, by the power of a Trinity in Unity. Chemistry teaches us, that this power of a Trinity in Unity is an all-creating power ; and so far it is man's comprehension of the creating power or Deity, and not a thing or principle incomprehensible : it is a doctrine older than the Christian era ; was a doctrine among the Pagan Philosophers, and is true as to principles or powers ; but not true in our modern sense of persons, as identical and separate beings.

A great mistake, too, has been made in the understanding of the word *person*, in relation to theology : it never was meant to express beings in the image of you and me ; but the dramatic manner of presenting a description of the principles of nature in the theatre, *per sonantem,* by sound or song, by fiction, by disguise, by allegory, by mask or mystery, by representative action : the revelation of which would be to understand the principles of nature so personated on the stage, as I have defined the Trinity. And it is in this, and no other sense, that I read the names of Deity in the Old or New Testament, as brought apparently on the stage of human affairs, in person, by the authors ; that *personating* meaning nothing more than a present picture or representation of an absent or

infinite power, by sounds or voice, and some-
times by masks, as was the earliest known
practice in dramatic exhibition, which explains
everything about gods and oracles, and makes
the Hymns of Orpheus as sacred as the Psalms
of David; as they are as certainly beautiful in
poetic composition, and equally useful to human
welfare.

You, Sir, if you enter the House of Commons
next month, may be said to *personate* the Electors
of Tamworth; a power in the abstract greater
than you, because many and supposed qualified
to reject your personation and to elect another.
Therefore, the personation is not the power personated. As the King's chief Minister, you will
also *personate* the King's Government in the
House of Commons; but you are not in reality
that governing power; because, it is something
distinct from you, and greater than can be con-
centrated in your person. You, as plain Robert
Peel, and I, as Richard Carlile, are not persons;
and though it is a custom so to use the word
and so to describe us, yet it is a mistake and
misuse of the word, unless the body may be
said to personate the mind, soul, &c. I hope
you see that much of the error of our Church
has turned upon this point; because a person
was never the reality of the power, and consequently the persons of the Trinity are not to
be considered the reality of the Trinity: and

hence the Unitarian Dissenter has no reasonable ground of dissent. The doctrine of the Trinity, as a description of Deity, is a valid theological and philosophical doctrine, admitting of no rational dissent.

I wish the Bishops to learn this before the Dissenters, so that the Church may be taught how to call back her errant and ignorant children, that her property may be held together for useful purposes, and not be wasted at the shrine of dissenting ignorance or bankrupt government.

And now, Sir, can you yet see your way with me, " to remove every abuse that can impair the efficiency of the establishment; extend the sphere of its usefulness, and strengthen and confirm its just claims upon the respect and affections of the people?" If you cannot, I beg you to follow me farther.

It is not only in physics that the doctrine of the Trinity is theologically and scientifically correct, but in morals also; and this is the foundation of the Christian Religion.

As God, the Father, *personates* all science, under the attribute of omniscience; that is, personates all existence, both omnipotence and omnipresence, and is, in that reality, the fountain of knowledge—the all and every part that can be known; so God the Son, Christ or Logos, personates the human mind, as the existence or manifestation of knowledge and reason, as Jesus or the principle of salvation from evil, in possessing that knowledge, and as the true God, in us and with us, in and with whom we live, and move, and have our being.

So God the Holy Ghost, the Spirit of Truth, the Comforter to come, to complete the happiness of the human race, personates that spirit of free communication of knowledge which should be found in the Church, the theatre, not of any superstition or dramatic ceremony, but of the freedom of the human mind, and all its emanations of free enquiry, free discussion, mutual instruction, which are the necessary elements of brotherly love and peace, in the proving of all things and holding fast that which is good. And thus I prove the truth of the doctrine of the Trinity.

This, Sir, is a true picture or effigies of the moral Trinity of the Christian Church, which you will find to be a key to every mysterious sentence of the Bible; and I ask you seriously, as between man and man, is any thing of this kind known or practised in the present Church? Are not the ministers of that Church afraid of every new discovery in science? Have they not, as far as they could, persecuted every man who has attempted to publish any criticism, enquiry, or objection to their mysterious subjects? History says—*Yes.* And I say that they have known nothing of the subject for themselves, and that they have dreaded all knowledge of, all enquiry into, the subject. Will their pride let them learn of me? Well may I say :—" Come unto me, all that labour and are heavy laden, and I will give you rest. Take my yoke upon you, and learn of me : for I am meek and lowly of heart : and ye shall find rest unto your souls. For my yoke is easy and my burden is light." That is the language of the personated Logos, or Principle of Reason, addressed to the present state of British mind, as it was formerly addressed to the general state of the human mind.

The doctrine of the transubstantiation of bread and wine, as the elements of the Sacrament of the Lord's Supper, into the real body and blood of Christ, has been another stumbling-block in the Church. On this head, our law-established Church has dissented from its former self, which when I mentioned on my last jury trial, the Judge, Sir Allan Park, called it a vilifying of the Church. I knew better; but saw that the Judge was not a man to be reasoned with, and so I did not press the subject : but through this letter and your name, Sir, I desire to teach him how it has been done. Transubstantiation is no stumbling-block to my mind.

The twenty-eighth article of the Church says on this subject :—" Transubstantiation (or the change of the substance of bread and wine) in the Supper of the Lord, cannot be proved by Holy Writ; but is repugnant to the plain words of Scripture, overthroweth the nature of a Sacrament, and hath given occasion to many superstitions. The body of Christ is given, taken, and eaten in the Supper, only after an heavenly and spiritual manner; and the mean whereby the body of Christ is received and eaten in the Supper, is Faith."

It is very clear to me that the Bishops of that time, the sixteenth century, did not know how to read Holy Writ. I could defend the entire doctrine of transubstantiation, in its fullest application, from the language of the Gospel according to Saint John. This subject affords me another proof, that the doctrine of transubstantiation is much older than any of the books of the New Testament: for, where understood, there is nothing in theology more clear than this doctrine, or that comes nearer to a physical and moral truth.

First, let us understand that the root of the word *Sacrament* is a secret in the mind; and *Transubstantiation* is a change of substance from one to another thing. Now the secret in the mind is, where understood, and where not understood there is no Sacrament, that, like the Trinity, all the appearances of God are in the principle of transubstantiation or change from one to another thing. All is motion.—Nature knows no rest. All is change, all is transubstantiation. It is like the Trinity,—one of the attributes of Deity, one not to be doubted,—because everywhere visible. The present Church of England calls it a damnable doctrine; but it is so called through ignorance. Like that of the Trinity, it is a doctrine much older than the Christian era; and so also was that of the Lord's Supper, as a practised ceremony.

When the name of Christ was set up to personate all the attributes of Deity, the various names of the Pagan gods were decried. It had become a matter of wisdom thus to set up the name of Christ as a personation of all the gods and goddesses: it was a concentration of philosophy, to unite mankind in one form of religion and for one great purpose, that of progressive and perpetual improvement. The plan was good; but the principle has never been rightly developed. Teaching by mystery is a bad system. The mass of the people are not so to be taught. We must begin and teach by revelation. The Christian Religion, when revealed, will be eternal, and realise all its real promises of peace on earth, good-will among men, and a land flowing with milk and honey.

Before the name of Christ was used, Bacchus was called a Saviour, as were many other if not

all the gods, as Jehovah is declared the only
Saviour in the Old Testament. And this Bacchus had the name of Jesus, or Saviour, inscribed
on his altar pieces, in the very letters now inscribed in our Churches, the three Greek letters
Iota, Eta, Sigma, I.H.S., not Jesus Hominum
Salvator, in initials, though so in meaning; but
YES, which is the same as Jesus, and signifies
Saviour. Isis is of the same root, one of whose
names was Ceres. Ceres personated corn or
bread, and Bacchus personated wine. It was a
Pagan custom, in religious ceremonies, to break
and eat bread in honour of Ceres, and to pour
and drink wine in honour of Bacchus, as the
bread and wine or body and blood of salvation,
of both physical and moral salvation.

Christ being made all, both physical and
moral Saviour, was intended to swallow up all
the various Pagan honours and ceremonies,
every one of which, in part or whole, is still
retained in our law-established Church; and
so Christ personated both the elements, bread
and wine, as his body and blood, as before they
had been called body of Ceres and blood of
Bacchus.

Be it remembered, that the Pagans had no
other ideas of these matters, than those of dramatic effect. The origin of the drama was in
and with the religion of the human race. And
we must come back or come up to this for a

right understanding and use of the Christian Religion.

As food, bread and wine are the best elemental representatives of the body and blood of the human being, and will sustain human life in health and vigour. As bread and wine, they are elements of the physical nature of God; and when taken into the human body, they transubstantiate in that body, and, in making blood, become the blood which is necessary to sustain the moral god or reason in the godly man: so, through the transubstantiation, they do not cease to be the body and blood of Christ. This is what is meant in the matter, and this solves the language of Saint Augustine, cited in the twenty-ninth article, that though the wicked eat the consecrated bread and drink the wine, they do not eat the real body and blood of Christ, because in leading bad lives they do not improve themselves, and so eat and drink but for new condemnation.

The revelation of the mysterious word *sin*, in the Sacred Scriptures, is generally applicable to the ignorance of the human race; and so of original sin, which is not to be otherwise reasonably understood. Man is born without knowledge, but may, by due care, be made a member of the Church of Christ; that is, may be made a scholar, as the foundation of a wise and good man.

I shrink not from a full and reasonable explanation of every part of the mysterious doctrine of the Christian Church, in this way; and I am prepared to maintain, before all men, that this is the true revelation of the mystery, the true spirit of the letter, both of the Old and New Testament: "the truth as it is in Jesus"—in nature: the truth, by God.

This beautiful and deeply-woven allegory embraces, in its mystery, almost every known process of nature; and must, in my opinion, have been the labour of the united science of many generations of the wisest men—of truly inspired men. This very doctrine of transubstantiation in the Sacrament of the Lord's Supper, is descriptive, and is in fact and principle, the death, burial, and resurrection of Christ in man. The bread and wine are swallowed, are buried in the human stomach, there decomposed or transubstantiated, formed into chyle, rise again into blood, and form the spirit of the man: which is, in reality, a death of the body and resurrection of the spirit: and the brain being the chief of the sentient principle, there becomes an ascension into that kingdom of heaven, which it is in a reasonable man, and than which there can be, by law of nature, no other. The same or similar explanation applies to the first and second birth; the birth of the physical body in its original sin, the second the birth of the spiritual mind or inward man, which is the Lord Christ Jesus. It is a divine riddle, and such is the solution.

The riddle is of larger comprehension than the mere relations of God to man. It is an astronomical almanack, a written and dramatized picture of the celestial globe; and is, in truth, a most perfect allegory of all known nature, both in physics and morals, in matter and spirit. There are no such men in the Church now as the writers of the Sacred Scriptures; none even with sufficient knowledge to understand them. We have fallen; yes, we have fallen into the dark ages; and the revelation, when known, is to be the millennium. We have fallen by that Scarlet Whore, the Babylon of Mystery; and have to rise again, by getting a knowledge of Christ, which is not now in the Church, nor yet among any of the Dissenters so called. Nothing can be imagined more anti-Christian in spirit and character, than that which has been called the Christian Church of the last fifteen hundred years.

Christ, in his physical character, personates the sun and solar year, while his twelve disciples personate the twelve months, or the signs of the zodiac; and, in this sense, we have a death, descent, resurrection and ascension, once a year. It is in that sense he performs the miracle of turning the water of the pot of Aquarius (January or

Winter) into the wine of Autumn ; the story, of course, is told, in the gospel, after the form of a personated narrative of a dramatic incident. So the product of the corn-seed of five small loaves and two fishes, becomes sufficient, in the season, to feed five thousand. The knowledge and ingenuity of the state of mind, that could so construct the allegory, as an harmonious picture of the works of nature, is absolutely wonderful, and has my admiration, even my ejaculatory adoration ; and I am not a little proud of my own ingenuity, in having penetrated thus far into so deep and mysterious a subject. It has brought me perfect peace of mind, as to the general system of nature, and left me burning with the desire to acquire more knowledge.

In the Church now existing, is there aught but mystery that can be called its religion ? And in mystery unexplained, unrevealed, can there be aught but impudent knavery in the ministration, with general hypocrisy or credulous folly in the reception ? I have penetrated the subject so deeply as not to shrink from saying, that the present ministration of the Church is an impudent and mischievous imposture, sanctioned by the custom of antiquity, that neither instructs nor moralizes the people ; for, notwithstanding all the pretences to religion, greater immorality than is here found cannot be supposed to exist among a people holding or held together as a community, in daily danger of disruption, and utterly without a code of moral guidance or guides: and this not so much among the poor as among the rich. Even this city is in danger, from its ill-assorted and ill-conditioned population, of all the disasters that befell Babylon, Jerusalem, Rome, Constantinople or Paris. And almost every village in the Island groans under want, and courts even the desolation of contested revolution for a change. And that very feeling and profession, which is now miscalled the religion of peace, will, from its state of ignorant dissension, only serve to whet the appetite for contention and slaughter, and make another war in the name of God.

I call upon you to repent, by which I mean reflection. I ask you to be honest, and that, too, because the season of profitable dishonesty is exhausted, and you have wealth enough: save it. It is never too late to reform and do justly; but the later the reform is deferred, the more necessity that the justice be rigid and prompt. I feel that if 1 had your authority, I could save the Church and its property, not for a farther career of its iniquity and error, but as a noble institution for the good of the people, a sufficient school for all, and a hospital for the infirm; to which, I add, that this, or nothing good, must have been the purpose of its first institution. I believe, from what I now see of the foundation of the Christian Religion, that this was the first purpose of its institution. Banish the superstition of the Church, plant the tree of knowledge there, and you will quickly overthrow the morally pestilent Dissenters. I mean, of course, by moral means, by the exhibition of more knowledge and wisdom and utility than they. This would be salvation and reform to every good institution in the country; for when knowledge becomes the nation's religion and moral pole-star, everything good is safe, everything evil will vanish before a discussion of its merits. This or blood-thirsty contention is your choice. You may delay for a while; but you cannot otherwise reform. You, by delay, will merely bid the people wait until they are strong enough to combat your authority. Delay will be a challenge to them of physical combat.

What can confer more dignity on the " Dignitaries of the Church " than for the Legislature to say to them :—" Feed the people with knowledge and no longer fill them with superstition ?" If I understand human nature rightly, it has more pleasure in honesty than in dishonesty.

Would the experimental lectures of a Faraday desecrate the building? Or a beautifully reflected picture of the heavens and its explanation lessen true devotion? Would moral science profane the pulpit or injure the congregation? Would the real catechism and instruction of children in matters of physical and moral science be of less importance than the parrot-like catechism of the language of the present mystery? There would then be some ground for a bishop's or overseer's examination and confirmation; but what does confirmation now mean? All that I can remember of it is a learning to repeat from memory a prayer and a creed, perhaps a few commandments, which are studied to-day, to be gone through to-morrow, and neglected ever after. Give the people something which they can feel and know to be useful, which they can reduce to practice, and they will emulate each other in flocking to Church at the appointed times. You will then have need of still more churches to receive the increasing population. It will be an emulative pleasure to children, a new delight to parents, a mutual gratification to be at school together in church.

I can say from observation, comparison and experience, that among the most moral of the working people in the metropolis, will be found those who have attended scientific lectures on the Sunday, and who have thereby been taught to contemn superstition. You find them not in the house of intoxication; but passing soberly in the evening from their homes to the school; and gratifiedly after the lecture from the school to their homes. The greatest error

that toryism and superstition have fallen into
has been to suppose that knowledge will make
a people disorderly. Bacon's aphorism is true,
that superstition is the *primum mobile* of sedition,
the great agitator; and ignorance the great
disorderer of States. Is it not so in Ireland?
Is it not your greatest trouble in this island?
The wisest act of the life of the late Lord Cas-
tlereagh was to propose to send *Paine's Age of
Reason* among the Roman Catholics of Ireland.
If it had been so thoroughly done, when he
proposed it, they would have been all quiet
enough by this time. Real knowledge is the
water-cup of sobriety for a people: with that
they will seek to rid themselves of nothing but
error and evil that cannot be morally defended.

Make the change that I propose in the business and ceremony of the Church, and you instantly make a Christian Religion, eminently
Catholic, that will not only annihilate the Dissenters, but convert Jew, Mahometan and
Pagan. It will be irresistible to all mankind.
They cannot argue against science; but each
argues against the superstition of the other.
Science is the essence of Judaism, but the men
called Jews understand it not. It is the foundation of their name, the ground on which they
have been considered a chosen people, it is the
only sign of God in man, the only proof of true
religion. Science and morals are the whole

duty and all needful to man ; beyond which he can gain nothing but superstition, error and evil. Science and morals, then, are the only proper business of the Church. Let us have our National Education in the Church. Let the Church be the fountain of knowledge, and all be there baptized, as a true sign of mental birth and membership of Christ.

Gather together all the property that was ever ecclesiastical; get it back from whoever may hold it; take it out of the hands of the priesthood or the ministers of the Church, tithes and all; and give it into the hands of its true owners, the people, each parish with its separate share, and let the majority of the parishioners make the best use of it they can for ecclesiastical, that is scholastical purposes; and with it, also, provide for their infirm and accidentally poor. This one act of public justice and public good would go far toward settling the affairs of this distracted and unsettled nation, and do injury to no one. Let the State Parliament be also the Church Convocation, which may be well done when there are no superstitious diputes, all will go on smoothly with due and sufficient authority and order, and Britain look forward to happy days. It would be the regeneration of the whole earth in a few years. This is what is meant by the promise of the knowledge of the Lord covering the earth as the waters fill the ocean.

Somebody must publicly break through the trammels of superstition, I have done it as far as a private man can do it ; but no public man in England has yet dared to approach the subject. Be you the first. No other circumstance could bring you a more imperishable name and fame. Of wealth you have enough. I ask nothing more than that you fulfil the promise of your administration made to the Electors of Tamworth. If you say, that you did not mean what I express, I shall answer you, that you could have no other meaning. Were I in Parliament, I would carry the subject in spite of prejudice ; so strong is my faith in the power of knowledge. I would move, in such a clear and simple way, that a man should not hold up his face to his fellow man after voting against me.

Give us a commission, with power to enquire into this subject. I will be content to wait all the time that justice to all concerned may require. If religion be any thing more than I make it—mental cultivation from infancy to death, it must be the private business of every man's life and nothing national ; like national sobriety, it must be made up of the sobriety of each individual, and cannot rest on social forms and ceremonies. Ceremonial sobriety would be but the mockery of a good principle. I care not how much repenting and proving we have, how much trial, let us but have free, full, and fair enquiry and discussion, in Parliament and out of Parliament. Giving a man knowledge cannot be a disqualification for true religion. Feeding him with science can have no tendency to injure his morals. Occupying his time well can be no source of bad habits. Spurring him on to a moral emulation in the acquisition of equal or more knowledge than his neighbour, will not create ill will toward that neighbour.

The best occupation of time is a question at the very root of individual happiness and national prosperity: I find it everywhere sadly neglected; here in prison, out in church, at the theatre, in public and private business, in families, in pursuit of pleasure, in the army— everywhere. It can be scarcely said, that there is anything solid in our actions; frivolity prevails everywhere, and is mixed up with our most serious professions. I cannot look back to Pagan times without seeing that they were a superior people to ourselves, and that we have fallen, through the management of our religion and politics, from, rather than risen, above them: we exceed them in nothing but hard and lengthy labour for small wages, insufficient for the necessaries of life. We have not learnt from Seneca, " that he lives longest who has made the best use of his time."

Be it your study to seek to give us some sound moral reforms, and sink party politics in the moral of public good; withdraw all licences from houses of intoxication and late hours; let there be no public resort, in Parliament or elsewhere, after ten at night; if it would be no abridgement of general liberty, confine shop business to limited hours, that the conductors and assistants may have due time for mental improvement. Some of the young men and women in London shops, bitterly lament the want of more time for rational recreation, for health and improvement. They are among the veriest of slaves in confinement. Let knowledge be once legislatively encouraged, remove all taxes from it, and then a hundred minor arrangements, by legislation, may be made conducive to public good, and a bar be set against injurious, offensive, and slavish competition. It is the Tory fear—and, in justice, I will add, Whig fear too—of knowledge that has produced all the present wrongs and evils of the country; for if cunning men have legislated, it has not been done for the public good; because there has not been sufficient public responsibility.

This is all Church as well as State business that I am proposing. The clear distinction as to Church and State is—that the Church means the people, congregated for mental improvement; and the State means the exercise of that mental improvement in their public business: so true it is, that Church must precede and give character to the State.

Tithes are a recognition of the original pro-prietorship of the whole people in the land; a rent paid under that consideration, appropriate-able to the sustenance of the poor, and the mental improvement of all.

Church Property is the property of the whole people who constitute the Church; and not, as now, of the ministers, who profess to be, and ought to be, the servants of the Church. At present, the servants are set above, defy, and tyrannize over the masters. All public officers in Church and State, from the King to the Beadle, should be subject to the periodical elec-tion of an intelligent people: without this, there can be no just and dignified authority—no pro-per public officers,—all will be tyranny, cor-ruption, and inefficiency!

In thus stating my subject, I am not insen-sible to the state of mind and conflicting in-terests with which you have to deal: but you are in a dilemma, from which nothing but wisdom and honesty can relieve you; every false or inefficient step will weaken you; any attempt to patch the holes made by Time in the mystery of the Church, will be like the tinker's work of mending one and making two: it is rusty and rotten, and must be knocked to pieces and burnt up, to produce the brilliant revelation from its ashes! There can be no mixture of the mystery with the revelation. The latter is a spirit that will explode the former; and, if you be a good Christian, let me tell you that the advent of the revelation will be the fulfilment of the promise of the gospel. We have had nothing but the mystery, nothing but the dark ages of ignorance and superstition : the mystery is not Christianity ; the revelation alone, which we have not had, is Christianity. The mystery and the revelation are as unlike each other, as the grossest superstition is unlike reason.

What a delightful state of society do I see before me, when the watchword of all shall be— GET KNOWLEDGE! The Bible abounds with this exhortation ; tells us all our disorders are lack of knowledge ; and yet we have been through centuries, almost through millenia, studiously and tyrannically keeping each other blind and ignorant. This has been the reign of the devil, Anti-Christianity, and not Christianity. When the portico of each Church-building shall bear the inscription of — KNOW THYSELF, AND ENTER HERE TO GET KNOWLEDGE, the communicant will see a friend in his minister, and the minister will strive to raise up wisdom in his communicant.

Now what do we see? Studied ignorance, and suppression of knowledge with both : each ashamed to look in the face of the other. And wherever a man advances beyond the existing state of mind, and publishes his sentiments, he is persecuted as an outcast, and unrelentingly subjected to prison-discipline, since the law has ceased to make the " offence " capital.

The unrevealed mystery of religion has been the curse and moral devil of the human race. A statesman cannot be wise and honest without setting his face against it, and seeking to rid of it the minds of his countrymen. With it, a state can have no permanent peace, nor can statesmanship be an honour. If you are not master of this subject, I am; if you will not press it upon the attention of the country, I will; and I have not a doubt, but that, by its superior moral power, it will enable me to succeed you in office. I invite you to take the task in your hands, and I will be content to be anything, to remain in prison, if this great reform be but put in motion while I live.

It is simply to begin to teach the people something useful in the Church, to give them useful knowledge, as easy in practicability as it is for a ripe scholar to become a schoolmaster to uninstructed youth. We have teachers all prepared for the purpose in the Clergy themselves. You have now to deal with a suspected and not a respected clergy. Though the great mass of the people do not understand where the fault theologically lies, yet they have instinctive discernment enough to see, that the relation of their condition to that of the Clergy is not founded in honesty and social utility. As sure as I, who see through the whole subject, the people feel that they are not fairly dealt with by the Clergy; and thus feeling, with such a Clergy, there can be no social peace. The feeling will increase as they get knowledge on the subject, and I have thrown that knowledge into the market, in defiance of all the power you have possessed or can possess; and that knowledge you cannot withdraw from the market of human intellect: the whole people will get at it in time.

Your boast is now that of being chief or leader of the CONSERVATIVES. This is not what the nation wants. It needs purgation of error, abuse and wrong, and a *restoration* of all the first principles of its Institutions. It is a fair question to put to you and your party, if you know the first principles of the Institutions of this country? You certainly have seen none of them in practice; for your scholarship and administration have been full of error and wickedness. As I told Sir Allan Park, that the Church had dissented from itself, so I now tell you, that every Institution in this country that is a thousand years old in name, has dissented from itself, and has, in fact, been changed diabolically—which means directly opposite, or from good to evil; and there never was a country whose cup of iniquity was more filled.

Conservation means preservation, and there is nothing in the present Institutions of this country but public wrongs and private abuses to be preserved. The name of a Destructive is far more honourable, in the present state of the country; the only name indeed that can be honourable, if it be interpreted, an intended destruction of error and abuses, of which the country is brim-full, and the fermentation pouring over.

I dislike all these names. They are all dishonestly used. They form no real distinction between man and man. The word *Radical* has always been to me an offensive word; the more particularly so as I have seen some very bad and ignorant men making a great noise under it and about it. We want knowledge and honesty to make it practicable, and no names by which to be distinguished: such names spring from ignorance and dishonesty.

The origin of our ancient Institutions has its foundation laid in the moral of law springing from the law of morals; and the restoration would be easy, if existing authority would resign itself to the change, or if it could be overpowered and made so to do. One or the other of these changes is necessary, before anything can be done, and the first the wisest and to be preferred. I believe there was a time when they existed without a mixture of any kind of deception

practised upon the people, and that is just what
I desire to see restored ; and which, I am sure,
from the growth of knowledge and criticism, is
the one thing needful to keep the country in a
state of inward peace.

Knowledge is the only spiritual interest of the
people : it should be fostered, promoted and
increased in the Church ; so as to be equalized
as far as possible among the mass or greater
number. The ignorance of the people has been
an excuse for many an act of hypocrisy, deception and tyranny : its continuance is now the
fault of the Church, and of those who have its
direction. Cunning cannot invent an assumption that any qualification can better serve the
spiritual and temporal interests of the people
than knowledge. Their degree of knowledge
is the all that is spiritual or of good within
them. It is an affair, too, where honest bro-
kerage is scarcely probable ; because no check
can be kept upon it. What, therefore, is not to
be defended as knowledge is not of God but of
the devil. In that sense, I arraign the whole
Church as now constituted, and challenge it to
stand a trial. I fear it is now too corrupt even
to be militant.

Let us suppose you about to attempt a reconciliation with the present Dissenters, as to the
doctrines and ceremonies of the Church. To
please the advocates of adult baptism, you must

exchange the infant for adult baptism, and then you will displease those who are not pleased with adult baptism. To please the Unitarians, you must give up the doctrine of the Trinity; and then you will displease all the Trinitarians. What is to be done to satisfy the Wesleyans or Methodists? They will have irregular prayers and preachings, which are contrary to the discipline of the Church. What is to be done with the Swedenborgians, the Muggletonians, and Southcotians? How can you furnish spirit and noise enough for the Unknown Tongues of the Irvingites? And what but the spirit of silence will conciliate the Quakers? All of them will require the abolition of your bishopricks and other offices, while none of them will object, and all will claim if a chance offer, to divide the Church Property among them. The spirit of dissent, in matters of religion, prevailing in this country, is nothing more than an infectious mental disease: with it, there is no reason mixed. The moment it becomes a profit to lead such a congregation, men of comparative talent as to capability will take it up and lead; and thus the thing has gone on to confusion and mental distraction, because the Church was not in a condition to defend itself and set a better example. You cannot please one sect of the Dissenters, without increasing the displeasure of the other: and thus your task is hopeless, on any other ground than that which I propose, to beat them in the superior communication of knowledge.

On the other hand, let us suppose the Church of England to begin to reveal the mystery of Jesus Christ, which I define, and maintain, to consist of a cultivation of the human mind, with all possible knowledge and reason; all other Churches must instantly bow to its superiority. The effect among men throughout the earth would be wonderful and intellectually electric. It is the only system that can be imagined to be a Catholic Christianity, and the very thing that is meant by the word *Catholic*, something alike suited to the welfare of every man, and which presents the principle of a moral equality, which is the only foundation for true liberty, and the only guarantee for an improvement of public morals ; one that would make the Church an attraction to the wisest as well as to the most ignorant of men ; those as teachers, these as learners.

We may carry the idea farther ; and as in the present state of mind, millions in Europe and America are attached to an idea of the superiority of the Church authorities at Rome, through ignorance and custom I grant, but not less attached,—I would, to humour that conceit and turn it to good, consent to make the Pope of Rome the centre of communication from all parts of the earth for discovered knowledge, as it would be desirable to have such a central recipient and fountain to give it forth again in the best possible manner. This would accelerate the reconciliation of the dissenting race, without an idea of dishonourable submission on the part of an individual. Indeed, the perfection of my proposition is, that no man can feel injury or degradation in the change. It is an overthrow of nothing, but simply the development and better understanding of the mystery that has existed since the world of human intellect began : the revelation of that mystery ; and, consequently, the completion or carrying out of the true Christian scheme.

It is not to be expected, that, in a pamphlet letter, I can do more than briefly notice a few leading points of this important subject ; but I am quite prepared to extend it through volumes, and shall go on so to do. I am quite prepared to meet or be one of any commission on the subject. I would willingly put my life upon the hazard of verifying my present views of original Christianity. It would have been done in former ages, had the printing press existed. Its doing now is consequent on the gradual power of criticism which the Press has brought with it into existence. It is the truth, and must prevail. It is the God in man. It is the Church of Christ, against which the gates of Hell shall not prevail. They have certainly prevailed against every other existing Church, and the whole of the past is a wreck.

When speaking of the original Christian
Religion, or of the revelation of the mystery, I
wish to be understood, as not meaning that the
revelation was ever before preached or openly
taught to the human race on any part of the
earth. We have no evidence of it beyond the
reasoning and moral precepts of the philosophical world, which were not put forth as a
scheme or system of religion. But when it is
confessedly the fact, that something called a
Christian scheme has been talked about for
eighteen hundred years; and when we can
trace the *fac simile* of that something, even in
its whole nomenclature, principle and practice,
through Greeks and Romans, Persians and
Hindoos, up to the Celtic Druids and earliest
known universal worship of Budha, the first
personation of Jesus Christ now on record;—I
mean, that the mystery has been the only general public part of it, and that the knowledge
of the revelation was confined to the learned
class and ancient mysteries of all countries, was
the esoteric doctrine of the initiated into those
mysteries; and the breaking up of those mysteries, from the time of Alexander to the Augustan era, was the cause of the first publication
in writing of the books or traditions handed
down through the agency of those secret and
sacred Associations, bearing the mystery only
on its surface and by the letter; and that after
the mystery was so published, the very ministers

of it lost the revelation, which is what the **Free-masons** profess to be in search of, the lost word, the word that I have found and now declare, that the salvation by Jesus Christ is only to be found in the increasing cultivation of the human mind with all attainable knowledge; that the true *worship* of God has no other meaning, the root of the word *worship* being to *cultivate*, and the field to be cultivated the human mind; that repentance is reflection for improvement; the second birth is the birth of mind, as distinguished from physical birth or birth of body, the one describing the man Adam, the other the God Christ; and that the kingdom of Heaven is to be established upon a general knowledge and practice of this revelation, is to be upon this earth, in successive generations of the human race, and not reasonably to be sought under any other speculation, calculation or hope. These are not only possibilities but probabilities, and immediate practicabilities, if the existing Devil will be pleased to retire: if not, we must resist him, and, as we are promised, on that condition, he will flee.

Such is the foundation of a Catholic Church, from which there can be no dissent; for what is understood cannot be dissented from: the existing dissent is ignorance dissenting from ignorance. In the common use of the word, I am not a **Dissenter**; but a trier, prover, teacher, revealer of that which is the true meaning of the mystery that has been through ignorance the cause of the dissent. The personation of Deity in the written mystery has been nothing more than a drama prepared for stage effect, which, to the initiated only, would be matter of instruction or refreshment of memory. The ancient mystery meant a play, a drama, in our modern sense; but was first called a mystery, then a morality; was first private, and afterwards made common to the public, and is now for the first time revealed to the general understanding, through the instrumentality of the printing press.

In my lecturings and discussions, both in town and country, I find this revelation has a great charm among all classes who have good temper and good manners to hear patiently. It is pure reason, pure knowledge, pure translation of language; it clashes with no other man's knowledge, and I have not found the man who can raise an argument against it. Of its final and complete success in regenerating the world, I have not a doubt; it is only a question of time. It is now a question, if you and the Parliament will look at it. I know you well enough to know, that you will not like its propounder; but who else has been ripe and bold enough to do it? Who else deserves the honour of being its propounder; but I, its honest martyr and zealous student, through a ten years' imprisonment? I call you to witness my fidelity in this matter. I was your prisoner through four years; you sanctioned the two years I had suffered before you came to the Home Department: you sanctioned my imprisonment by Lord Melbourne, through thirty-two months: and, by virtue of your office, you are sanctioning my present imprisonment. I do not say this in anger. I am retaliating upon you, as I would have you retaliate upon the Dissenters, by superior knowledge. If you do not now or early take me by the hand, I shall drive you out of the field of politics, and all who may succeed of your disposition.

It is not to be denied, that there are moral exhortations put forth in every Church; the mystery would not pass on the people without them. But it is a truth, that, in all of them, morals are treated as a secondary consideration; and in some of the madder dissenting Churches, are counted as of no weight in the question of religion. The truth, as it is in Jesus, is, that *morals are every thing as to practice*, and knowledge with succeeding reason, the principles of speculation, the WORD to be sought, or the prize to be gained, the crown of glory, the spiritual and immortal life, which is emphatically the language of Saint John's Gospel; and this is the totality of the root and principle of the Christian Religion, the promotion of which is the only proper business of the ministration in the Church. No mystery : down with mystery. It is the folly of the human race, and worse than ignorance, or knowing, or confessing to know, nothing. There is no Christ in the mystery. "How can we reason, but from what we know?" The knowledge must be first. Nothing precedes knowledge but the thing to be known. Nothing is required after ; but a dealing with the thing known by principle of reason. Unknown worlds, unknown spirits, unknown matter, is nothing to us, until the knowledge is obtained. Our knowledge is our all, in moral power, and we can have nothing of a religious nature but our knowledge. Superstitious fears, we know to be the property or sensation of ignorance and misconception. We are morally responsible for nothing but an improper use of our knowledge. It is wickedness to teach ignorance any other doctrine.

My Christian proposition for the Reform of the Church harmonizes with all science, and clashes with nothing but positive error and wicked policy ; and I venture to tell you, that you can find no other scheme to produce the same effect, and to give satisfaction to the present and to all future generations of men, to make the Church " meet the respect and affections of the people."

Each paltry sect now considers its tenets as a

Catholic Faith; but the truth is, as Dr. Geddes well observed, "that what is Christian is Catholic, and what is Catholic must be Christian;" but then, this follows, that neither Christianity nor Catholicity will bear a union with the word *dissent*, unless the dissenter be an intelligent corrector at the same time: they are adverse to every admissible idea of undiscussed dissent. All standing dissent is of the devil; while Christianity and Catholicity are of God and Heaven. The multiplication table, the elements of Euclid, the doctrines of the Trinity and Transubstantiation, the proved analysis and composition of all known substances, are Catholic doctrines, from which nothing but ignorance can dissent. The whole of the present Church Ritual is a mass of words that conceal a truth; but that truth is not known in the Church, cannot therefore be used or worshipped, and the words can only be deemed the lumber of the memory: treating man as man treats a parrot, teaching him constantly to exclaim "pretty Poll," without giving him understanding whom or what "Poll" personates.

If I were to sit in Church through a morning or evening service, I should have a perfect understanding of all the words used, and, consequently, should be worshipping according to the limit of THE WORD there presented; because I have in me the spirit of revelation.

But this is not the case with those who now attend the Church, their attendance is upon form, ceremony, mystery, hypocrisy, which is the real meaning of the whole present business of the Church : hypocrisy, or dramatical acting, set forth in a mystery, without a mixture or accompanying revelation ; and like the flimsy gildings of a theatre, or the spangles of an actress' dress, gilded over with a little moral exhortation, that you may observe or not, as you please, so as you are a cheerful payer of all dues, rates, and oblations. The first revision wanted in the Church is a translation of the revelation from the dead language of its mystery, into language comprehensible by all. Consequent upon such a revision would be, that the parishioners would take the management of their own Church Property into their own hands, and recover and hold **THEIR MOST SACRED RENT OF TITHE**, on recovery of the knowledge that they are the first and inalienable proprietors of the land.

My subject is so far novel as to justify a little repetition. That twice two is four need not be repeated ; but where the human being is enveloped in a cloud of verbose mystery, that cloud can only be dispelled by continued flashes of moral lightning. So I will return to methodical statement.

The mystery of the existing Church, in all its

grades of dissent, having set forth and caused the belief of a temporal and local existence of the personated principles of Deity, as distinct and separate from ourselves, in imitation of the Pagan Mythology, and not as simulated beings; it is requisite, as matter of proof, sooth and truth, that a case of clear human history of the circumstances be first made out, the doing of which my knowledge, after trial, challenges; and if that could be done, the more difficult task would remain, to prove, that such beings, the authors of such circumstances, as could be historically proved, were super-human. If the first cannot be done, the clumsy mystery falls to the ground, as the Dagon of the day, before historical criticism : and if the first be done, and the second cannot bear the light of scientific and philosophical criticism, the mystery is still but a mummery, which belief can no longer prop, nor physical power farther propagate; it is thrown into the crucible of moral criticism, and men will not longer consent to believe that the same causes will demonstrate differing effects, nor that varying causes may be made to demonstrate the same effect.

I have read in public prints of your creditable attendance at the Royal Institution of Albemarle Street, on the demonstrative Lectures of Mr. Faraday in the Science of Chemistry. When there, were you asked to believe anything?

Was not everything demonstrated, so that the words were verified by the acts of the Lecturer? If Mr. Faraday had played you *hocus pocus* or legerdemain tricks, as a pretence of chemistry, would you have been satisfied? If he had told you of strange and incomprehensible things, which he could not demonstrate, would you have believed?—I think not: I give you credit for a better state of mind. Take a lesson from the inference, and grasp this truth, that the Royal Institution in Albemarle Street is the best Church in the country, and is, in reality, the nearest existing approach to the Catholic Church of Christ. It would be rational, it would be wisdom, if all were spending their Church-time at such lectures, who are old enough to receive such instruction.

I hope it will not offend you, nor be an untruth, to. say, that you learnt something on every occasion of attending Mr. Faraday; that you, a Secretary of State, there found you had something to learn; and that a field was there opened to knowledge, which would, had it pleased you, before all other occupation, have wisely and usefully engaged the whole time of your remaining life. On the other hand, in the spirit of truth and charity, but of free enquiry, allow me to ask, if you could ever say the same, after an attendance at Church, on leaving, that you had learned something that was, without pretence, matter of real learning, an acquisition in knowledge possessed, that was not previously known in your school-hours and as a matter of school-business, or that might not have been learned from a book at home?

I extend the question, in asking, whether anything that may be taught a boy at seven years of age, is improved on, by an attendance on the present state of the Church to seventy or four score years of age? If not, and I say—*No*, to what good purpose does this expensive establishment exist? Or, may it not be put to a better purpose? and if it may, why not? To talk about Church Reform, without doing something that shall tend to a full amount of practical and permanent good, is to insult the Nation; because the existing state of the Church is really a burthen and a grievance, and of no general utility.

No Church was ever reformed by and with the consent of its Priesthood. I am of opinion that the Bishops and Clergy ought not to be consulted in this affair :—they are not the Church ; but the ministers or servants of the people, which form, or ought to form, the Church. A Royal or Parliamentary Commission, with unlimited powers of enquiry, is the first power necessary with which to commence this subject of Reform in the Church.

If we did not know human nature, history

affords the warrant, that the Bishops and Clergy generally will follow the profits of the Church: those in the reign of the Tudors changed back and forward five times from Catholic to Protestant. But under this proposition of mine, what dignity is evident in the change! Instead of making the Bishops overseers and the Clergy generally actors of a drama, I purpose to put the whole structure of the human mind under their superintendance and guidance: not to be dealt with as now, but really to be educated in all attainable knowledge. My purpose is as practicable as that any other person can teach any kind of knowledge. Give the human being a better occupation of time, let the human mind expand where it may, and you guarantee perpetual peace and improvement, with dignity to every class of men, with injury to none.

The change which I propose will be tantamount to a national change from diseased and crippled infancy to healthy adolescence. General man has not yet had fair play. No Nation, the history of which is known, has made a real effort to promote the happiness of all its members. Class has preyed upon class; idleness has been claimed as a privilege on one side, and slavery, through force, been made an inevitable duty on the other. For the furtherance of such a state of society, superstition has been encouraged, that a pompous class might be

decorated to preach submission among the la-
bourers to the Spirit of Tyranny and Imposture
that was riding riotously over them. There can
be no liberty and solid happiness among a superstitious people; and all attempts, at what is
called political reform, that leave the people
mentally rotting in superstition, will be abortive.
I take credit for one fact—that there has been
no change made in the political spirit of this
country through any other medium than warfare
with superstition; for the baneful and blighting
spirit of that superstition admitted not of the
thought of any other change.

There is a glimpse of light latent to show
that all the monastic institutions, the temples,
the abbeys, priories, convents, nunneries, the
mysteries, the churches, synagogues, and ora-
tories, were originally instituted as schools of
useful knowledge; and for what other good
purpose could they have been instituted? The
better part of the human mind is now making
an effort to restore the purity of that state of
things. Nothing short of this can tend to har-
monize the human race in their several nations,
with this improvement upon the past, that all,
and not a class only, be educated. It was this
education of a class only that has created all
the mischief of superstitious society. The class
educated has imposed untruths upon the un-
educated class, until education itself to that class

became swallowed up in imposture; and now both preacher and hearer may be truly said to be alike ignorant of all the great truths that are important to man, and necessary to social welfare. In the way in which the Bible is now read, after being printed, no preachers or teachers are necessary: to have been taught to read is sufficient. Give every man his Bible from Church Property, after teaching him to read, and the present Church business is completed: but much otherwise is my view of the subject. There is not a man living that has now a thorough understanding of the contents and meaning of the Bible. Many are working for the restoration of its lost science; and it is a subject worthy of a Church.

It may startle a First Lord of the Treasury into new thought, to be told, that neither of the Books of the Bible is a piece of human history, not a history of beings like you, me, or any one else. I have given up all idea of the kind as untenable and indefensible. It may startle the Chancellor of the Exchequer, who is supposed to have the counting or reckoning of millions of money yearly, and contemplating that Giant of Despair—the Debt, to be told, that the Bible is fundamentally a mathematical book; and that he who does not so understand it, understands it not at all, or but in a very small degree, as to its moral bearing. The Duke of Sussex can give you an opinion on this head, as to the Bible being a book of algebraical science; though, perhaps, he would not like to say it applied to astronomical motion, and was a record of time so calculated through myriads of ages. A Bishop should understand this. It is a book of much more importance than has been made of it in the last thousand years in England. If the Bishops were required to have studied this book before they took office, we should find them generally as lean and as sallow as a lawyer who has to wade through the statutes at large, and law reports as large, for his sort of knowledge; a knowledge that I do not like, and will have none of, but what is forced upon me. No kind of knowledge is requisite to make a modern Bishop. The very origin of the title of a Bishop is that of an astronomical seer, a looker-out or overseer of the subordinate offices of science. There is a plenty of work, so as to allow of no idleness in any office of the Church, if justice be done to the people; and I will not grudge a thousand pounds a-year as a salary to a competent Bishop, or even more than that, if the Property of the Church will afford it. Ignorant fools they must have been, to have allowed so important, so honourable and dignified an office to become corrupt, and to fall into disrepute among the people.

This algebraical reading of the Bible subdues

all idea of contradiction to any science, geology for instance, chemistry or any other science, as well as of the apparent language of the book in letter to letter. For instance, the letter-objecting Infidels have laid great stress on Moses being set forth as having seen God ; when the author of the Gospel according to Saint John says :—" No man hath seen God at any time." This is ignorantly set down as a clear contradiction. The explanation is, that *Moses was not a man;* and then there is no appearance of contradiction. One is mythologically, and the other morally, true.

The Hebrew and Greek alphabets, being numerical as well as literal signs, which was probably the case with all other ancient languages, and these accumulating large numbers, by additional points, it is impossible that we can have a clear understanding of the meaning of their mythological sacred books, without a full algebraical knowledge of the language ; and this explains how the letter killeth or stupifieth, while the spirit or knowledge of the entire meaning alone giveth life or understanding. The deepest investigators of the Hebrew Bible of this day maintain that it should be algebraically understood as a book of astronomical science—as a record of time by astronomical motion, which, physically speaking, can alone be the WORD OF THE WORKS OF GOD.

The only true religion must be founded in man's reasonable comprehension; all other pretences to it are presumptions and nonsense to be condemned. We may as properly speak of religious horses and cows, as of men who are ignorant of the subject, substance and meaning, of what is religion. Saint Anthony's preaching to fishes is not without its simile in the practical part of that which has been mistakenly called the Christian Religion. That which is in practice, under the name of the Christian Religion, among many grades of Dissenters, is a disgrace to the government of the country, and to the name of civilized society: it grows worse and worse. Madness is beginning to be added to mystery; or is now produced by the mystery without the key of revelation. Through revelation there can be healthy excitement and enthusiasm; but none through mystery.

Our King is not now the head of a Church, nor the King of a People: he can only be truly described as the head or King of Dissenters, which is an office much more troublesome and dangerous than honourable. To his Ministers, the present state of religious mind must be a prolific source of trouble; and has, I believe, made them persecutors, where the inclination of their own hearts was not coincident with the act. The Dissenters are now much less tolerant than the law-established Church; and if they

are not undermined by my proposition, it will
not take them many years to undermine that
Church, or to demand a share of its property.
To be able to see this, it is only necessary that
we be acquainted with the workings of human
nature, where not under the controul of knowledge.

I am not content that the Established Church
shall stand merely as one among Dissenting
Churches ; no Minister of State should be so
content: the King is thereby dishonoured,
and the State in disorder. I would have it a
Church morally dominant and militant against
all error, as it always should be, and as it was
in the beginning. The meaning of the word
militant has been entirely lost, in the growth of
mystery and decay of revelation in the Church.
There is a great talk now about revelation, or
of something revealed in the Church ; but there
is no reality in the revelation. There is a mystery pregnant with revelation ; but not in itself
the revelation. It is a fountain of knowledge,
but the genius of man must draw it out. It is
good for nothing, but has caused a world of
mischief, where read and understood as merely
by the letter, as we read an ordinary book of
history. The Church now wants the revelation
or spirit. Not one of those existing has a particle of spirit.

My proposition for a Reform will anni-

hilate infidelity as well as dissent. **There is**
no infidelity toward knowledge. **It has been**
ignorance all through, on both sides, **that has**
raised the cry of infidelity : each has been
unequal to teaching. The Infidel has rejected
that literal reading which the professing be-
liever could not defend ; because he did not
understand its relation, as mystery to revelation.
Both, in fact, have been alike Infidels. If I
have been the chief of Infidels, I will atone for
it in becoming the chief defender of revelation,
and the faith, as it is in Christ Jesus, and not
as it is in any Dissenting Church. Already the
ignorant Infidels murmur at what they mistakenly call my apostacy, while no member of
any existing Church holds out a hand to my
welcome.

As the Church goes now, it is not required
that its Ministers be learned men : they have
nothing to do for which talent is requisite—it
is a mere school-boy's task ; and even among
the Dissenters, where the prayer and preaching
is extemporaneous, it is not learning, but memory and habit, that are required. In the
Church, as I would have it reformed, not only
learning but talent to teach would be necessary ;
and the Ministers would rise to Bishoprics, not
through family or political interest, but through
preparation and capability to fill the office ; for
it would be required of them to be first-rate

scholars and practical men in display of science, that sort of science, too, of which they are now so much afraid—the unlimited knowledge of things, rather than of languages.

In what class of ages do we place the dark ages of man's history? To whose account are they placed? To the Pagan, Jew, Mahometan, Infidel, or whose? I blush for the Church when I consider it—to the account of that *misnomer*, the *Christian Church!* So your pretended light to lighten the Gentiles, made them all darker, did it? Yes, it did and does, as your Church has mistaken it! And none of you are yet out of the fog created by the mystery. Not one of you has gained light of mind sufficient to dispel a particle of that fog of the dark ages. You are all, as Churchmen, as dark as any of those who lived in the tenth, eleventh, twelfth, or any other century; talk about your Reformation, Printing Press, Bible Societies, Dissenters, or what you please! The admission which has been made, not by the adversary, but by the Church itself, that the dark ages are within its reign, is decisive of the question as between me and any who may oppose me. Let it not be said, that the fault was in the Roman Catholic Church, and that it has been removed. I deny the assumption; the fault is not removed, nor has any Church made the least improvement on that called Roman Catholic. The fault lies in

the remaining unrevealed mystery of the Church
and the Sacred Scriptures. As far as Church
is in question, this Nation is as dark as ever it
was, and such is the case throughout Europe.
There is much thick darkness to be yet dispelled; before our gentility is enlightened. We
are precisely in the same error as the Hindoos,
to whom we send Missionaries; and though we
talk about civilization, we have it not. Our
general state of society would shock the moral
feelings of an American Indian. There are, in
reality, but two distinct states of society : the
superstitious and the civilized, the dark and the
light. Can any man reasonably say, that we
have yet passed the superstitious state? Are
we not rather in the very depth of it ; the light
of a few individuals, now and then visible, acting
upon the whole like flashes of lightning on a
dark night, are seen and spent quickly, lost or
buried in the general darkness, though effects
may be left? The liberty which I have won in
prison, to make the printing press bear upon
this darkness, is the first unextinguished light
that has been set up and kept burning. I now
desire to light the seven candles of the English
Church from my lighted torch. I would not be
presumptuous if I saw any other man putting
himself forward to propose this necessary business. It is not in me conceit : it is a passionate
desire to do good and to leave the world bet-

ter than I found it. So many years of imprisonment (this being the tenth) must shorten the period of my life, so I grow the more anxious to do the more while I remain *a bubble on the sea of matter borne.* Not that I despair of eternal life, but I learn from the Gospel that I must provide it for myself.

In the present state of the Church, there is no sufficient and satisfactory motive given for keeping holy the sabbath-day; there is no reason given for holding a sabbath. I state it as a necessary civil institution for the improvement of the human mind, since labour to live is the condition of life. While the honest labourer is following his social avocation through six days, I would have his children going through a course of education by the Ministers in the Church, their especial office—" suffer little children to come unto me, and forbid them not; for of such is the kingdom of Heaven ;"—and on the seventh, or sabbath day, I would have such discourses, such teaching in the Church, as should be suitable to the united presence of both old and young. This would be a satisfactory motive to keep that day holy ; and such, as far as I can see, was the evident purpose of the Sabbath and of the Christian Church. No other use of the Church can be more hallowed ; no purpose more sacred ; no employment more dignified to the minister as well as to the people. When Peter, in the Gospel, is called upon to feed the lambs of Christ, what was meant?—to feed them with grass? No! to feed the infants of the Church with true and useful knowledge; not to do which is treason to society and breach of trust in the Ministers of the Church. Oh! here is a fine field open, in which the lambs may gambol and grow up in spiritual stature, without living to be led like sheep to the slaughter! Knowledge is the proper business of the Church, and the people's only spiritual interest; and this is the foundation of a Catholic Church and of a Christian Religion, that is to bring peace on earth and good-will among men, which have not yet been seen, notwithstanding the supposed promise of the mistaken mystery for the last seventeen hundred years, so many centuries of a sinking state of things, of a fall of man from the light into dark ages! Let there be light in the Church and the people shall be enlightened. The true Church is now eclipsed by the mystery, and is a dark body. The knowledge of the revelation will be the extinction of the mystery, the light of the Church, and the salvation of the people from war, pestilence and famine.

That revelation, according to the gospel itself, I take to be, that, as knowledge is the only distinction between man and any other animal, the more can be acccumulated for him in the Church, the more good will be done, and the more he will be saved from evil. Existing things can alone be the subject of man's knowledge, and it is of more importance to him to know their properties than their time or history. Now, nothing of the properties of existing things is taught in the Church; but through the medium of the mystery remaining unrevealed, unexplained, or untranslated in our language, every thing is falsified to man's credulous view and consideration, by the ministers of the Church; nature appears to him distorted, and he lives without certainty, and dies deceived as to the future. Knowledge is as infinite as existing things, and man's power of acquisition illimitable. It is, then, a proper labour and business, and moral duty, of each generation of men, to leave behind them, for their successors, the largest possible amount of knowledge. This is true wealth, and will increase the value of all other wealth : without knowledge, other wealth is mere animal gratification. The spirit of knowledge gives life and new properties to everything, as far as man's use of it be in question. The Church is the proper fountain of this knowledge; should be the public library, the parish laboratory for investigations, the school for infants and adults, and everything that is auxiliary to the acquisition and extension of knowledge. From all I can trace, 1 verily believe that such was the original purpose and construction of the Christian

Church; and that back to this it may be easiest and best reformed.

I am confirmed in the opinion, that putting knowledge under the form of an allegorical mystery, for the purpose of confining it to a class, has been the cause of the mistake and its declension, and of the scholar's fall from a former higher estate of knowledge. Decidedly do I conclude, that our stock of knowledge is much below the quantity possessed some two or three thousand years ago, when the holders of the sacred books held the revelation with the mystery. I am sure it may be recovered, if fairly and earnestly sought. I see an impulse gathering over both Europe and America for the recovery of that knowledge. The Church was instituted to become the repository of knowledge; and all would have gone on well, but for the ancient system of deceiving what were and are called the vulgar—of having a double doctrine, the exoteric and esoteric, telling the people one thing and understanding quite another among themselves. Such were deceivers and not teachers of the people; and though the revelation has really been lost, lost, I may say, as a just punishment for the wickedness of so deceiving the people, the successive Clergy has been ignorantly deceivers and not teachers of the people. They have inherited the exoteric or mysterious doctrine, and have

not inherited the esoteric doctrine or the revelation of the mystery. This they have to learn,
before they can reform their Church, or, before
any one can reform it for them.

I am confident enough to say, that you have
no other ground on which to reform the Church,
than that which I am proposing. Whatever
other step you take will only be an aggravation
of the evil of which you have now to complain ;
or of which others complain. If the Bishops
have one item of wisdom among them, they will
take me by the hand, and put their houses in
order this way : if not, you and they may dis-
sipate the existing Church Property, which you
say you will not do; and after, we shall begin to
form such a-new, and recover what we can of
that property. I shall not despair of taking an
active part in this thorough Reform of the
Church while life remains : the People can do
it for themselves, if Clergy, Ministers and King
will not consent. It is what I began to do in
my house in the year 1828, in critical and philosophical lectures and free discussion on the
Sunday : an example which I am happy to see
followed in many parts of this metropolis, and
which will go on, if it be not cordially met, until
it swallows up the Church and all the Churches.

The true meaning of Church, is STATE OF
MIND. Church is the state of mind. It is not
made up of building and clergy ; but of the

people, the proper depositaries of mind. Property belonging to the Church is property belonging to the People, sacred to the preservation, strengthening, and increase of mind or knowledge. It has been monopolized dishonestly by the Clergy ; and, in that sense, they have been robbers as well as deceivers of the people. This is the matter to be reformed, and nothing short of this will be reform. In Tithes, the people stand as the original proprietors of the land, the true inheritors of its tithes and first-fruits. Other rent is a minor consideration of value in labour or capital bestowed on the land. We must come back to this by some means or other.

The office of King, as head of the Church, is a clerical office—the crown both of the Church and the State ; and, for the sustentation of its true splendour and dignity, the man or woman filling the office should be the first scholar and most wise and virtuous being of the Nation. Whether this is a principle to be conveyed by hereditary descent, I do not stop to enquire ; but the true hereditary principle of church office is talent and moral character ; upon which, I doubt if any improvement can be made for purposes of state. Originally, in this island, Church and State were but one. The branching into two has been the result of wars and evil passions, to distinguish between the instructive and the destructive offices. A hierarchy founded upon knowledge would be equal to all that society wants as government. State, as well as Church, signifies the People. As the latter relates to their minds, knowledge, or spiritual affairs, so the former expresses their politics and civil arrangements, their local and temporal affairs: they may be well united in one common interest, and under one common authority, in the reign of a people devoted to the acquisition of knowledge.

It is matter of curious observation to see how the use of names among political parties is abused, and how they get reversed in applicable meaning. The class that has lately taken the title of Conservatives, is the class that, by the showing of this letter, has been destructive of everything valuable in our Institutions, so that we have the name only left, without any virtuous principle that formerly existed in those Institutions. We have the evidence of this in all the present difficulties of the country, both in Church and State. The ancestors of this class have not known how, or not cared to preserve those ancient Institutions in their original purity; and the class now wanted is the class of Restoratives, of men whose knowledge, wisdom, honesty and virtue, will enable them to purge out the accumulated errors of centuries, and restore the Institutions of the country to their pristine purity. I grant that this class is not found among the men who are commonly called or claim to be called Radical Reformers: there is as much ignorance in that class as in any other. But they certainly are not likely to be more destructive than they who call themselves Conservatives; for these have left nothing to be destroyed. The true and real aim of the men now called Radicals is to begin something a-new. Their profession of respect for existing Institutions is hollow, hypocritical and deceitful. I have had acquaintance enough with them to know that; and more than for the reminiscence of which I can now find respect. Still they will supersede both Tory and Whig, if these do not something upon the principle of a true restoration of Institutions to original and best principles. I would have the Radicals treated as the Dissenters: leave them no ground of complaint, and so annihilate them. A wise King or a wise Minister would see that the time is now come at which that step should be taken, and that further delays will be dangerous to every man in office. Necessary Institutions, if destroyed for a time, will rise again. I fear no kind of change as to the prospect of future advantage.

Is not the idea horrible, and of the worst description, that a Church and King, or Church and State, should exist and hold together on no better tenure than a military power; than that of an army constantly under arms to keep the people from carrying their complaints to an extent disagreeable or alarming to the men in office? Yet such is all that you can boast of in the present state of the Institutions of the country. These Institutions did not originate under the protection of an army; nor did they, at their origination, require an army to protect and keep them in existence. An army is a disgraceful appendage, and destructive of every good principle in the Church:—it is not an honourable appendage to the office of King. To the people, it is a burthen and an immoral pest; less requisite in this island than in a continental nation. Give the people knowledge in their Churches, and they will soon dispense with an army.

Evils accumulate because there is error at the bottom. There is now no People's Church: it is, as now existing, a Church of the Clergy, engrossing and wasting a large property of the people's due to a most valuable social purpose. The Dissenters have only made the matter worse, in new exactions for no new benefits. Not one tittle of good, not a particle of utility, now proceeds from the Clergy toward the people. They are obstacles to the people's welfare, and their use of means of provision for a new and better Church.

God is the subject of man's adoration. But what is God? Man is but an idiot if he professes adoration beyond his understanding. Indeed, *worship* is but a synonyme of *reason* and its cultivation; and as we say:—*how can we reason but from what we know?* so we may as truly say:—*how can we worship what we do not know?* There is no worship without knowledge; all other pretence to it is idolatry and superstition. I have not space to enter upon this topic largely here; but a voluminous treatise on the word GOD will be the subject of my next Essay. For the purpose of this illustration of what the Church is, and what it ought to be, I can say correctly, that God, as the aggregate of existence, is known to be a physical and moral power. We have distinct ideas of this two-fold power. The American Indians, who speak of God as a Great Spirit, make the best general definition of the word that can be made, and appear to me to have the clearest, purest and wisest idea of Deity, as far as the regulation of their actions by that word is in question,—the pursuit of knowledge, by the use of letters and figures excepted. It corresponds with the emphatic declaration of the Gospel according to Saint John, chap. iv., v. 24 :—" *God is a Spirit, and they that worship must worship in spirit and in truth;*"—which means what I have before stated, that they must know what they worship before they can worship. There is evidence of physical as well as moral spirit. Both are seen in man, and constitute what may be termed the Spirit of Man. The one in man is worshipped or cultivated by attention to health; the other by attention to mental improvement or increased acquisition of knowledge. Speaking of God, as the aggregate and source of physical and moral spirit, of which man is a part or unit, we experience that we cannot alter our physical construction, or physical spirit, other than by attention to rules of health in the law of nature; but we can, by study and labour, greatly alter the state of mind or moral spirit. It is here we draw from God as from a fountain; and this asking, seeking, drawing from God, constitutes the whole principle of right prayer and worship, and the structure of the true Christian Church; other than which, I declare, is worship of the Devil and not of God. And I do not shrink from saying, that, as revelation is light and knowledge of God, and mystery is darkness and presence of the Devil, there has not through the last fifteen hundred years, the dark ages, throughout Europe, been carried on any other kind of worship than Devil-worship, and evil has been the fruit thereof. It was under this knowledge that I was moved to exhibit the effigy of the Devil arm in arm with the Bishop, in the front of my house and in several prints, for which

I am now suffering imprisonment, like all other martyrs to truth, punished for acting upon my knowledge. My purpose was good, to open the eyes of my neighbours and passers by. It might have inconvenienced some of them ; but such is the effect of every newly-published truth in eradication of error: your Reform of the Church, be it what it may, will inconvenience the Bishops and some of the Clergy. There would be no Devil, if there were not pleasure in Hell as well as in Heaven ; as pardon can be had by asking for it. If all evil were naturally punished, we should not want penal laws.

As true worship is a getting of a knowledge of God, so it follows, that the Ministry of the Church should consist of a teaching that knowledge, which is not now the case; for nothing as knowledge is in the Church taught.

There can be nothing more clear in mathematical demonstration, than that, as God is a Spirit, of which man may partake, the participation must increase with that only which can increase in man—the amount of his knowledge. The whole declaration of the Christian Creed, read by the spirit, is, that God is the Spirit of Knowledge, the thing known, the principle of omniscience; and that man approaches and lives with God, as his mind expands in the accumulation of knowledge. A Bishop may write or preach spiritually or metaphysically by the

year, and he can make no more of the word
God, of his Church, or of himself, than I have
made. The subject now wants a radical reform
in the human mind.

I have mentioned, in a former page, that the
Jews can trace no nationality to the time of the
Emperor Alexander of Macedon. The highest
antiquity that can be given to them as a colony,
is the time of Ptolomy Lagus, who began to
encourage science and literature in Alexandria ;
and, from that time, nothing but a colony could
they have ever been. It is not in a nationality
that the original character of a Jew is to be
estimated, but in a philosophic character dis-
persed among the nations ; a people devoted to
science ; and so a chosen or select, because a
learned people. There is no resemblance in
character between an ancient and a modern
Jew :—the name is an Asiatic name of God ;
and can only apply to a race of men in the
sense of having perfected human nature, which
it is very probable the ancient Jews had done,
as far as it was then possible to do it, according
to the system of initiation, through a series of
discipline, into all the schools and mysteries of
that time and country. The first public reference
to a stated existence of the Books of the Old
Testament is the reign of Ptolomy Philadelphus.
Egypt appears to have been the only country in
which it can be said that a series of Kings gave

encouragement to science, which appears, as far as history is witness, to have brought in the Augustan era. It became, as far as wars and tumults would permit, fashionable so to do, until superstition overwhelmed it and usurped all its names, leading on to the dark ages of what has been since mis-called the Christian era. Cultivation of science is the restorative power, and the only public or private act that confers true dignity on man. This is the only remedy for the disorder of the Church; and I have introduced this historical view of the Jewish name, to show how flimsy is that web of superstition which has been woven in the existing Church on the foundation of a supposed national history and origin of the Jews. Truth no where finds opposition in fact, date, or principle: error is opposed by endless proofs of the kind.

It remains now only that I give an outline of the historical defects of the present received view of the mystery of the Christian Religion, and then draw to a conclusion.

No record extant, or referred to, that, having been written in the first century, has mentioned the human existence of an individual of the name of Jesus Christ.

A passage now in Josephus is a declared interpolation, inasmuch as it was first known to the world in the Ecclesiastical History of Eusebius, written in the fourth century, after Photius and Origen, of the third century, had written, that Josephus had not made mention of Jesus Christ.

In the writings of Philo Judæus, an Alexandrian Jew of the first century, much is said about the Logos, in carrying out the philosophy of Plato; but not a word about Jesus Christ.

Pliny the younger, in his letter to the Emperor Trajan, written from Bythinia between the years 106 and 112, is the first to mention the name of Christ. This mention is as of a God and not as of a man; no reference is made to Judea or to Jews; and the worshippers of this God he describes under the name of Christians, and as having long existed as a sect in that province. He writes as if he had heard nothing of the sect at Rome, and describes their worship as an excessive superstition.

The passage in Tacitus is rejected, as not noticed by Eusebius or any one before the fifteenth century; that it was found in a copy by Johannes de Spire at Venice.

This brings us to Justin Martyr, who can only be considered a Christian of the Platonic order, making no reference to Gospels or Epistles.

Thence we come to St. Irenœus, Bishop of Lyons, who has very much the appearance of a Druidical Bishop rather than as a newly-appointed Christian Bishop. Irenœus mentions the four Gospels of Matthew, Mark, Luke and

John, and gives the reason why there should be four; as because there are four seasons in the year. He has many other allegorical extravagancies in his writings, and is not deemed the most respectable of the Fathers of the present Church.

In the third century, and toward the latter part of that century, near three hundred years after the supposed birth of the man Jesus Christ, we have a recognition of all the Books in the New Testament, which received the stamp of the authority of a Council of Bishops, as a selection from many similar and dissimilar books under similar titles, in the fourth century; but whether the revelation of the mystery was then understood by the Bishops does not appear.

The Epistles of the New Testament have no dates nor reference to any persons who were known to have lived at any particular time. They are not supported by, nor do they support, the Gospels. The idea of allegorism prevailed in the third century.

The Christian era was not reduced to chronology until the sixth century; and that chronology was very little used or referred to until the tenth, that the era of the Hegira of Mahomet had come much into use. The real struggle of the present Christian Church was not with the Pagan but with the Mahometan Religion, and they are near a balance of numerical power to this day. A battle in France, in the reign of Charles Martel, checked the progress of the Mahometans, and saved the entire overthrow of the mysterious Christian Church on the continent of Europe. There was a much greater similarity between the Pagan and the Christian, than between the Christian and the Mahometan Religion.

I have no objection to the religion of the Jew or the Christian, that is founded on the spiritual reading of the Bible. Mahometanism is superior to both, while founded on the reading of the letter. The restoration of the Jews to original character and the millennium of the Christians is only to be brought about by the spiritual reading, which will lead to a devotion to science. The future Temple of the New Jerusalem must be a Temple devoted to the promulgation of truth and all sciences, and such must be the Church of Rome, and such our English Church, under any real state of reformation.

The practical part of my proposition for a Reform in the Church, is, that all indefensible superstition or mystery be banished or explained, that it be made the best possible general school for the people, to which the knowledge of the time is equal ; that the people being the Church, and the Ministers not being the Church, the property of the Church in each parish shall be managed by the parishioners as their property, and the best provision be made with that property, including tithes, that can be made for all the physical and moral necessities of the people. The property must be put under some authority, cannot be allowed to remain as it is, cannot be well put under extra parochial authority; but may be well and honestly left to parochial management, as the property of the parish.

As our Institutions were all so first arranged for this purpose, so it will be found, that every thing emanating will fall back easily into its natural, moral, and original use. I cannot see the least difficulty, beyond the dishonesty and reluctance to yield of existing spirit. Such as are so weak in mind as to desire the present Church ceremony, may have it as long as they like, so as they do not exclude more useful business. I repeat, that, if the Bishops and Clergy be wise, they will take this advice: if they do not, they will very soon be where their predecessors were in the seventeenth century, not to be restored again.

I flatter myself, that, in this letter, I have produced a pamphlet that will not be deadborn. As far as possible, or as clearness of purpose would permit, I have endeavoured to avoid the use of offensive language. Whatever the world may think of me, I know nothing more of myself, than that of having a passion to be

——— to my country and fellow-men generally, ——— previous to the critical coming time of ——ange. It is not now to be mistaken as near. It is near, and very near. The present system may be dragged on through several years; but no one can insure it a twelve months' existence. I know that all bad passions are allied to ig-' norance, and I desire to see all those passions softened down by knowledge. I am sure that the new man, the spiritual man, the good and moral man, must be created by knowledge and independent individuality of action; and as I prefer (the Government having the choice) a moral to any other revolution, brought about by words rather than by harder and harsher wea- pons, I feel, that I have but performed a social, a civil, and a religious duty, in presenting this letter to your notice. That it may be read, marked, learned and inwardly digested, is the prayer of

Your humble Servant,

And prisoner in the business of Church Reform,

RICHARD CARLILE.

Giltspur Street Compter,
    January 29, 1835.
TENTH YEAR OF IMPRISONMENT.

26 JY 66

Printed by R. Carlile, 62, Fleet Street, London.